Veloce *Classic Reprint* Series

How to restore

Yamaha
FS1-E

YOUR step-by-step colour illustrated guide to **complete** restoration
Covers all models

More titles by Veloce Publishing

1½-litre GP Racing 1961-1965 (Whitelock)
AC Two-litre Saloons & Buckland Sportscars (Archibald)
Alfa Romeo 155/156/147 Competition Touring Cars (Collins)
Alfa Romeo Giulia Coupé GT & GTA (Tipler)
Alfa Romeo Montreal – The dream car that came true (Taylor)
Alfa Romeo Montreal – The Essential Companion (Classic Reprint of 500 copies) (Taylor)
Alfa Tipo 33 (McDonough & Collins)
Alpine & Renault – The Development of the Revolutionary Turbo F1 Car 1968 to 1979 (Smith)
Alpine & Renault – The Sports Prototypes 1963 to 1969 (Smith)
Alpine & Renault – The Sports Prototypes 1973 to 1978 (Smith)
Anatomy of the Classic Mini (Huthert & Ely)
Anatomy of the Works Minis (Moylan)
Armstrong-Siddeley (Smith)
Art Deco and British Car Design (Down)
Autodrome (Collins & Ireland)
Automotive A-Z, Lane's Dictionary of Automotive Terms (Lane)
Automotive Mascots (Kay & Springate)
Bahamas Speed Weeks, The (O'Neil)
Bentley Continental, Corniche and Azure (Bennett)
Bentley MkVI, Rolls-Royce Silver Wraith, Dawn & Cloud/ Bentley R & S-Series (Nutland)
Bluebird CN7 (Stevens)
BMC Competitions Department Secrets (Turner, Chambers & Browning)
BMW 5-Series (Cranswick)
BMW Z-Cars (Taylor)
BMW Boxer Twins 1970-1995 Bible, The (Falloon)
BMW Cafe Racers (Cloesen)
BMW Custom Motorcycles – Choppers, Cruisers, Bobbers, Trikes & Quads (Cloesen)
BMW – The Power of M (Vivian)
Bonjour – Is this Italy? (Turner)
British 250cc Racing Motorcycles (Pereira)
British at Indianapolis, The (Wagstaff)
British Café Racers (Cloesen)
British Cars, The Complete Catalogue of, 1895-1975 (Culshaw & Horrobin)
British Custom Motorcycles – The Brit Chop – choppers, cruisers, bobbers & trikes (Cloesen)
BRM – A Mechanic's Tale (Salmon)
BRM V16 (Ludvigsen)
BSA Bantam Bible, The (Henshaw)
BSA Motorcycles – the final evolution (Jones)
Bugatti Type 40 (Price)
Bugatti 46/50 Updated Edition (Price & Arbey)
Bugatti T44 & T49 (Price & Arbey)
Bugatti 57 2nd Edition (Price)
Bugatti Type 57 Grand Prix – A Celebration (Tomlinson)
Caravan, Improve & Modify Your (Porter)
Caravans, The Illustrated History 1919-1959 (Jenkinson)
Caravans, The Illustrated History From 1960 (Jenkinson)
Carrera Panamericana, La (Tipler)
Car-tastrophes – 80 automotive atrocities from the past 20 years (Honest John, Fowler)
Chrysler 300 – America's Most Powerful Car 2nd Edition (Ackerson)
Chrysler PT Cruiser (Ackerson)
Citroën DS (Bobbitt)
Classic British Car Electrical Systems (Astley)
Cobra – The Real Thing! (Legate)
Competition Car Aerodynamics 3rd Edition (McBeath)
Competition Car Composites A Practical Handbook (Revised 2nd Edition) (McBeath)
Concept Cars, How to illustrate and design (Dewey)
Cortina – Ford's Bestseller (Robson)
Cosworth – The Search for Power (6th edition) (Robson)
Coventry Climax Racing Engines (Hammill)
Daily Mirror 1970 World Cup Rally 40, The (Robson)
Daimler SP250 New Edition (Long)
Datsun Fairlady Roadster to 280ZX – The Z-Car Story (Long)
Dino – The V6 Ferrari (Long)
Dodge Challenger & Plymouth Barracuda (Grist)
Dodge Charger – Enduring Thunder (Ackerson)
Dodge Dynamite! (Grist)
Dorset from the Sea – The Jurassic Coast from Lyme Regis to Old Harry Rocks photographed from its best viewpoint (also Souvenir Edition) (Belasco)
Draw & Paint Cars – How to (Gardiner)
Drive on the Wild Side, A – 20 Extreme Driving Adventures From Around the World (Weaver)
Ducati 750 Bible, The (Falloon)
Ducati 750 SS 'round-case' 1974, The Book of the (Falloon)
Ducati 860, 900 and Mille Bible, The (Falloon)
Ducati Monster Bible (New Updated & Revised Edition), The (Falloon)
Ducati 916 (updated edition) (Falloon)
Dune Buggy, Building A – The Essential Manual (Shakespeare)
Dune Buggy Files (Hale)
Dune Buggy Handbook (Hale)
East German Motor Vehicles in Pictures (Suhr/ Weinreich)
Fast Ladies – Female Racing Drivers 1888 to 1970 (Bouzanquet)
Fate of the Sleeping Beauties, The (op de Weegh/ Hottendorff/op de Weegh)
Ferrari 288 GTO, The Book of the (Sackey)
Ferrari 333 SP (O'Neil)
Fiat & Abarth 124 Spider & Coupé (Tipler)
Fiat & Abarth 500 & 600 – 2nd Edition (Bobbitt)
Fiats, Great Small (Ward)
Fine Art of the Motorcycle Engine, The (Peirce)
Ford Cleveland 335-Series V8 engine 1970 to 1982 – The Essential Source Book (Hammill)
Ford F100/F150 Pick-up 1948-1996 (Ackerson)
Ford F150 Pick-up 1997-2005 (Ackerson)
Ford GT – Then, and Now (Streather)
Ford GT40 (Legate)
Ford Midsize Muscle – Fairlane, Torino & Ranchero (Cranswick)
Ford Model Y (Roberts)
Ford Small Block V8 Racing Engines 1962-1970 – The Essential Source Book (Hammill)
Ford Thunderbird From 1954, The Book of the (Long)
Formula 5000 Motor Racing, Back then ... and back now (Lawson)
Forza Minardi! (Vigar)
France: the essential guide for car enthusiasts – 200 things for the car enthusiast to see and do (Parish)
From Crystal Palace to Red Square – A Hapless Biker's Road to Russia (Turner)
Funky Mopeds (Skelton)
Grand Prix Ferrari – The Years of Enzo Ferrari's Power, 1948-1980 (Pritchard)
Grand Prix Ford – DFV-powered Formula 1 Cars (Robson)
GT – The World's Best GT Cars 1953-73 (Dawson)
Hillclimbing & Sprinting – The Essential Manual (Short & Wilkinson)
Honda NSX (Long)
Inside the Rolls-Royce & Bentley Styling Department – 1971 to 2001 (Hull)
Intermeccanica – The Story of the Prancing Bull (McCredie & Reisner)
Italian Cafe Racers (Cloesen)
Italian Custom Motorcycles (Cloesen)
Jaguar, The Rise of (Price)
Jaguar XJ 220 – The Inside Story (Moreton)
Jaguar XJ-S, The Book of the (Long)
Japanese Custom Motorcycles – The Nippon Chop – Chopper, Cruiser, Bobber, Trikes and Quads (Cloesen)
Jeep CJ (Ackerson)
Jeep Wrangler (Ackerson)
The Jowett Jupiter – The car that leaped to fame (Nankivell)
Karmann-Ghia Coupé & Convertible (Bobbitt)
Kawasaki Triples Bible, The (Walker)
Kawasaki Z1 Story, The (Sheehan)
Kris Meeke – Intercontinental Rally Challenge Champion (McBride)
Lamborghini Miura Bible, The (Sackey)
Lamborghini Urraco, The Book of the (Landsem)
Lambretta Bible, The (Davies)
Lancia 037 (Collins)
Lancia Delta HF Integrale (Blaettel & Wagner)
Land Rover Series III Reborn (Porter)
Land Rover, The Half-ton Military (Cook)
Laverda Twins & Triples Bible 1968-1986 (Falloon)
Lea-Francis Story, The (Price)
Le Mans Panoramic (Ireland)
Lexus Story, The (Long)
Little book of microcars, the (Quellin)
Little book of smart, the – New Edition (Jackson)
Little book of trikes, the (Quellin)
Lola – The Illustrated History (1957-1977) (Starkey)
Lola – All the Sports Racing & Single-seater Racing Cars 1978-1997 (Starkey)
Lola T70 – The Racing History & Individual Chassis Record – 4th Edition (Starkey)
Lotus 18 Colin Chapman's U-turn (Whitelock)
Lotus 49 (Oliver)
Marketingmobiles, The Wonderful Wacky World of (Hale)
Maserati 250F In Focus (Pritchard)
Mazda MX-5/Miata 1.6 Enthusiast's Workshop Manual (Grainger & Shoemark)
Mazda MX-5/Miata 1.8 Enthusiast's Workshop Manual (Grainger & Shoemark)
Mazda MX-5 Miata, The book of the – The 'Mk1' NA-series 1988 to 1997 (Long)
Mazda MX-5 Miata Roadster (Long)
Mazda Rotary-engined Cars (Cranswick)
Maximum Mini (Booij)
Meet the English (Bowie)
Mercedes-Benz SL – R230 series 2001 to 2011 (Long)
Mercedes-Benz SL – W113-series 1963-1971 (Long)
Mercedes-Benz SL & SLC – 107-series 1971-1989 (Long)
Mercedes-Benz SLK – R170 series 1996-2004 (Long)
Mercedes-Benz SLK – R171 series 2004-2011 (Long)
Mercedes-Benz W123-series – All models 1976 to 1986 (Long)
Mercedes G-Wagen (Long)
MGA (Price Williams)
MGB & MGB GT– Expert Guide (Auto-doc Series) (Williams)
MGB Electrical Systems Updated & Revised Edition (Astley)
Micro Caravans (Jenkinson)
Micro Trucks (Mort)
Microcars at Large! (Quellin)
Mini Cooper – The Real Thing! (Tipler)
Mini Minor to Asia Minor (West)
Mitsubishi Lancer Evo, The Road Car & WRC Story (Long)
Montlhéry, The Story of the Paris Autodrome (Boddy)
Morgan Maverick (Lawrence)
Morgan 3 Wheeler – back to the future!, The (Dron)
Morris Minor, 60 Years on the Road (Newell)
Moto Guzzi Sport & Le Mans Bible, The (Falloon)
Motor Movies – The Posters! (Veysey)
Motor Racing – Reflections of a Lost Era (Carter)
Motor Racing – The Pursuit of Victory 1930-1962 (Carter)
Motor Racing – The Pursuit of Victory 1963-1972 (Wyatt/Sears)
Motor Racing Heroes – The Stories of 100 Greats (Newman)
Motorcycle Apprentice (Cakebread)
Motorcycle GP Racing in the 1960s (Pereira)
Motorcycle Road & Racing Chassis Designs (Noakes)
Motorhomes, The Illustrated History (Jenkinson)
Motorsport In colour, 1950s (Wainwright)
MV Agusta Fours, The book of the classic (Falloon)
N.A.R.T. – A concise history of the North American Racing Team 1957 to 1983 (O'Neil)
Nissan 300ZX & 350Z – The Z-Car Story (Long)
Nissan GT-R Supercar: Born to race (Gorodji)
Northeast American Sports Car Races 1950-1959 (O'Neil)
The Norton Commando Bible – All models 1968 to 1978 (Henshaw)
Nothing Runs – Misadventures in the Classic, Collectable & Exotic Car Biz (Slutsky)
Off-Road Giants! (Volume 1) – Heroes of 1960s Motorcycle Sport (Westlake)
Off-Road Giants! (Volume 2) – Heroes of 1960s Motorcycle Sport (Westlake)
Off-Road Giants! (volume 3) – Heroes of 1960s Motorcycle Sport (Westlake)
Pass the Theory and Practical Driving Tests (Gibson & Hoole)
Peking to Paris 2007 (Young)
Pontiac Firebird – New 3rd Edition (Cranswick)
Porsche Boxster (Long)
Porsche 356 (2nd Edition) (Long)
Porsche 908 (Födisch, Neßhöver, Roßbach, Schwarz & Roßbach)
Porsche 911 Carrera – The Last of the Evolution (Corlett)
Porsche 911R, RS & RSR, 4th Edition (Starkey)
Porsche 911, The Book of the (Long)
Porsche 911 – The Definitive History 2004-2012 (Long)
Porsche – The Racing 914s (Smith)
Porsche 911SC 'Super Carrera' – The Essential Companion (Streather)
Porsche 914 & 914-6: The Definitive History of the Road & Competition Cars (Long)
Porsche 924 (Long)
The Porsche 924 Carreras – evolution to excellence (Smith)
Porsche 928 (Long)
Porsche 944 (Long)
Porsche 964, 993 & 996 Data Plate Code Breaker (Streather)
Porsche 993 'King Of Porsche' – The Essential Companion (Streather)
Porsche 996 'Supreme Porsche' – The Essential Companion (Streather)
Porsche 997 2004-2012 – Porsche Excellence (Streather)
Porsche Racing Cars – 1953 to 1975 (Long)
Porsche Racing Cars – 1976 to 2005 (Long)
Porsche – The Rally Story (Meredith)
Porsche: Three Generations of Genius (Meredith)
Preston Tucker & Others (Linde)
RAC Rally Action! (Gardiner)
RACING COLOURS – MOTOR RACING COMPOSITIONS 1908-2009 (Newman)
Racing Line – British motorcycle racing in the golden age of the big single (Guntrip)
Rallye Sport Fords: The Inside Story (Moreton)
Renewable Energy Home Handbook, The (Porter)
Roads with a View – England's greatest views and how to find them by road (Corfield)
Rolls-Royce Silver Shadow/Bentley T Series Corniche & Camargue – Revised & Enlarged Edition (Bobbitt)
Rolls-Royce Silver Spirit, Silver Spur & Bentley Mulsanne 2nd Edition (Bobbitt)
Rootes Cars of the 50s, 60s & 70s – Hillman, Humber, Singer, Sunbeam & Talbot (Rowe)
Rover P4 (Bobbitt)
Runways & Racers (O'Neil)
Russian Motor Vehicles – Soviet Limousines 1930-2003 (Kelly)
Russian Motor Vehicles – The Czarist Period 1784 to 1917 (Kelly)
RX-7 – Mazda's Rotary Engine Sportscar (Updated & Revised New Edition) (Long)
Scooters & Microcars, The A-Z of Popular (Dan)
Scooter Lifestyle (Grainger)
SCOOTER MANIA! – Recollections of the Isle of Man International Scooter Rally (Jackson)
Singer Story: Cars, Commercial Vehicles, Bicycles & Motorcycle (Atkinson)
Sleeping Beauties USA – abandoned classic cars & trucks (Marek)
SM – Citroën's Maserati-engined Supercar (Long & Claverol)
Speedway – Auto racing's ghost tracks (Collins & Ireland)
Sprite Caravans, The Story of (Jenkinson)
Standard Motor Company, The Book of the (Robson)
Steve Hole's Kit Car Cornucopia – Cars, Companies, Stories, Facts & Figures: the UK's kit car scene since 1949 (Hole)
Subaru Impreza: The Road Car And WRC Story (Long)
Supercar, How to Build your own (Thompson)
Tales from the Toolbox (Oliver)
Tatra – The Legacy of Hans Ledwinka, Updated & Enlarged Collector's Edition of 1500 copies (Margolius & Henry)
Taxi! The Story of the 'London' Taxicab (Bobbitt)
To Boldly Go – twenty six vehicle designs that dared to be different (Hull)
Toleman Story, The (Hilton)
Toyota Celica & Supra, The Book of Toyota's Sports Coupés (Long)
Toyota MR2 Coupés & Spyders (Long)
Triumph Bonneville Bible (59-83) (Henshaw)
Triumph Bonneville!, Save the – The inside story of the Meriden Workers' Co-op (Rosamond)
Triumph Motorcycles & the Meriden Factory (Hancox)
Triumph Speed Twin & Thunderbird Bible (Woolridge)
Triumph Tiger Cub Bible (Estall)
Triumph Trophy Bible (Woolridge)
Triumph TR6 (Kimberley)
TT Talking – The TT's most exciting era – As seen by Manx Radio TT's lead commentator 2004-2012 (Lambert)
Two Summers – The Mercedes-Benz W196R Racing Car (Ackerson)
TWR Story, The – Group A (Hughes & Scott)
Unraced (Collins)
Velocette Motorcycles – MSS to Thruxton – New Third Edition (Burris)
Vespa – The Story of a Cult Classic in Pictures (Uhlig)
Vincent Motorcycles: The Untold Story since 1946 (Guyony & Parker)
Volkswagen Bus Book, The (Bobbitt)
Volkswagen Bus or Van to Camper, How to Convert (Porter)
Volkswagens of the World (Glen)
VW Beetle Cabriolet – The full story of the convertible Beetle (Bobbitt)
VW Beetle – The Car of the 20th Century (Copping)
VW Bus – 40 Years of Splitties, Bays & Wedges (Copping)
VW Bus Book, The (Bobbitt)
VW Golf: Five Generations of Fun (Copping & Cservenka)
VW – The Air-cooled Era (Copping)
VW T5 Camper Conversion Manual (Porter)
VW Campers (Copping)
Volkswagen Type 3, The book of the – Concept, Design, International Production Models & Development (Glen)
You & Your Jaguar XK8/XKR – Buying, Enjoying, Maintaining, Modifying – New Edition (Thorley)
Which Oil? – Choosing the right oils & greases for your antique, vintage, veteran, classic or collector car (Michell)
Works Minis, The Last (Purves & Brenchley)
Works Rally Mechanic (Moylan)

www.veloce.co.uk

First published May 2006 by Veloce Publishing Limited, Veloce House, Parkway Farm Business Park, Middle Farm Way, Poundbury, Dorchester DT1 3AR, England. Fax 01305 250479 / e-mail info@veloce.co.uk / web www.veloce.co.uk or www.velocebooks.com. Reprinted November 2017.
ISBN 978-1-787112-52-0 / UPC 36-36847-01252-6

Readers with ideas for automotive books, or books on other transport or related hobby subjects, are invited to write to the editorial director of Veloce Publishing at the above address.
British Library Cataloguing in Publication Data – A catalogue record for this book is available from the British Library. Typesetting, design and page make-up all by Veloce Publishing Ltd on Apple Mac. Printed and bound by CPI Group (UK) Ltd, Croydon, CR0 4YY.

Veloce *Classic Reprint* Series

How to restore
Yamaha
FS1-E

YOUR step-by-step colour illustrated guide
to **complete** restoration
Covers all models

John Watts

VELOCE PUBLISHING
THE PUBLISHER OF FINE AUTOMOTIVE BOOKS

Enthusiast's Restoration Manuals from Veloce Publishing –

978-1-903706-44-2

978-1-903706-46-6

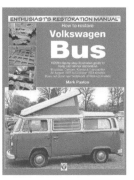

978-1-845840-93-8

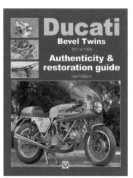

978-1-845843-18-2

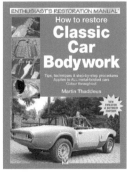

978-1-845843-18-2

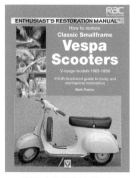

978-1-845844-37-0

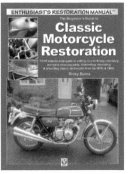

978-1-845846-44-2

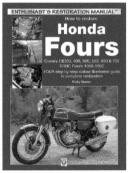

978-1-845847-46-3

978-1-845847-73-9

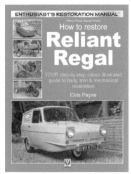

978-1-787112-51-3

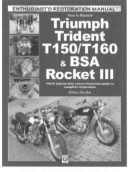

978-1-845848-82-8

978-1-845849-46-7

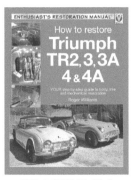

978-1-845849-47-4

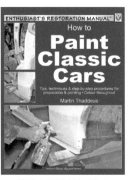

978-1-787111-42-4

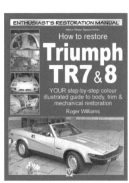

978-1-787112-52-0

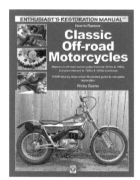

978-1-845849-50-4

978-1-845849-83-2

978-1-787110-28-1

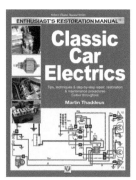

978-1-787111-01-1

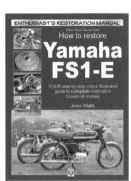

978-1-787112-50-6

Contents

Labour of love, complete.

Foreword by Andy Naughton-Doe

Teenagers, and especially sixteen-year-olds, by their very nature have an inbuilt desire to find out what makes things tick, and will prod, poke and dismantle anything mechanical at the drop of a hat. The teenagers that worked on their machines in the seventies, using pocket knives and can openers to remove generator covers and set timing, for example, will have created a great deal of work for the modern restorer.

The book that is set to help us with such a restoration has finally come along ... we needed it nearly 30 years ago (but probably would not have read it). Back in the 1970s, turning sixteen was a momentous thing. Kids had a year of this ham-fisted bodgery to obtain optimum performance (normally around 45mph on the flat but inflated to well over 60mph by the time it was discussed over an illicit pint). Then, before you knew it, the Fizzy was discarded for a ton-up Yamaha RD250LC, Suzuki X7, or even a Mk1 Ford Escort or rusting Mini, on or a few days after their seventeenth birthday. The Fizzy was either consigned to a scrappy (after a long and damp wait in the backyard), passed to a sibling,

or sold to another speed crazy sixteen-year-old. However, the number of people looking for their old Fizzy amazes me, even now after thirty-odd years.

When I first met John Watts, many years ago, I was taken aback by his depth of knowledge of the internal combustion engine, and of the Fizzy in particular. He had just unearthed a barn find and was systematically restoring it to its former glory. He had a number of other projects on the go at the same time, and I was impressed at his ability to juggle the various tasks involved. John's methodical approach to restoring and his attention to detail make him an ideal choice to write this guide.

Owning a Fizzy meant adventure! You could go anywhere, make new friends and impress people. My brother once went on holiday from Hull to Wales on his Fizzy. In those days that was an epic journey for a teenager, only made possible by the famous two stroke. I recently came across an article in a 1970s copy of *Bike* magazine, featuring a Fizzy road test from London to County Mayo in Ireland. Classic stuff and what an adventure!

Restoring a Fizzy is quite a task in terms of time and money. Hunting down new old-stock parts is all part of the fun and, with the advent of eBay, things have never been easier. The availability of genuine parts from Yamaha (for the time being at least) is a great help. Never give up hope of finding that elusive barn find. Many stories abound of people clearing out their garages, perhaps feeling guilty at letting their once pride and joy disintegrate into a heap of rusting scrap metal ... and just want to find a good home for it's rebirth.

Once restored, running, and, dare I say it, MoT'd, then the fun has only just begun. There are clubs to join, such as the Vintage Japanese Motorcycle Club and the Sports Moped Owners Club, and there are events and meets all over the world for all FS1s. For some people, just like in the 1970s, the restoration will evolve into obtaining optimum performance – but that's another story.

This book will prove invaluable if you embark on a restoration project, but even if you don't want to venture that far it will surely bring back memories of a long forgotten era.

Introduction & using this book

The picture on the left shows what the few remaining FS1-Es look like today. However, with a good restoration, they can look like the machine shown on the right.

INTRODUCTION

If you're reading this book, it's probably because you're one of the many people who owned or coveted one of the Yamaha FS1-Es imported into the UK between 1973 and 1978, the FS1 was sold all over the world until the mid-1980s. I, for example, saved up every bit of money I could from my Saturday job at Tippetts Motorcycles in Surbiton, Surrey, together with birthday and Christmas money, for two years so that as soon as I was 16 I could be the proud owner of my first FS1-E, registration number LGJ 685P.

Needless to say, I wrote it off within a month of having it by showing off with some mates. Tippetts sent me to Roy Smith Motors who provided me with second hand parts to carry out the repairs – the problem was paying for them! So it was back to Tippetts, earning the money for the necessary parts to get my bike as good as new. The knowledge and experience I gained at Tippetts whilst carrying out the repairs proved

invaluable at the time, and has helped me carry out my own restoration projects on my collection of FS1-Es.

During the four years since I took on my first restoration project, I've met many people all over the UK who are interested in this particular model of moped. Invariably, the people I meet are around the same age as me, anything from the 1957 to the 1966 vintage who, when I explain what I'm doing, either say, "I had one of those", or "I wanted one of those but my parents refused", or "my mate had one of those and he used to let me have a go". These exchanges are usually followed by conversations along the lines of what colour bike they had and that their particular model could go at 60mph flat out. Of course, those of you who know the FS1-E will remember that you had to lean flat, chin on the speedo and turn full throttle to get maximum speed, which by then usually made the engine scream.

Some of the FS1-E enthusiasts confess that they 'customised' their machines by painting them a completely non-Yamaha colour, cutting the pedal gear off, or tried to make them look like a later model by changing the tank, or the shock absorbers, and moving the ignition switch. Another trick was to discard the original tail light(!) and cut off the back of the rear mudguard and install a small tail light up behind the seat. The front mudguard would also be thrown away and replaced by a GRP mudguard. All of this is, of course, sacrilege to today's FS1-E collector.

In this book I will take you through the process of finding your own model and restoring it to mint condition. I will also guide you through the minefield of dodgy wrecks, so-called FS1-Es that are dressed up to look like the original, and how to source parts and materials to enable you to complete the job.

Most people who want an FS1-E now either had one at 16 or wanted one. For most previous owners, their FS1-E holds fond memories of their first taste of freedom and independence. From my experience, FS1-E owners remember a great deal about their bikes, including registration numbers and any minor modifications they made.

The market for FS1-Es has grown in the last few years. Many ex-owners, now in their late 30s and 40s, are looking to recreate their original machines. In the 1980s, FS1-Es would change hands for next to nothing, but now even a wreck is worth several hundred pounds.

Finding an FS1-E is quite a task in itself. I now own seventeen machines and most of them have either been

Beware, though, as you can get carried away!

bought on eBay or via contacts made following initial contact on eBay. Other machines have been bought through the FS1-E website, and others through classified adverts in motorcycle magazines. I've been told that placing a wanted advert can produce results but I've had no success with this method.

When looking for your FS1-E, in my opinion, the least important thing is overall condition. The most important thing is maximum originality.

It's important to decide on the model you want. My preference is the badge-type models, 1972 to 1976. This type has the screw-on badge tanks, side ignition and enclosed shock absorbers. Additionally, the front brake plate should be located on the right-hand side and the drive sprocket is separate from the rear wheel. Model differences are detailed later in this book.

Beware, though, you might get carried away. What starts out as a

What starts out as a simple hobby, can escalate into an obsession!

would be advised to obtain a parts list, a workshop manual, and an owner's handbook.

The Haynes workshop manual is an invaluable reference for looking after your FS1-E, and will also be of help to restorers. Although currently out of print, many copies of the various editions of the manual are still in existence, a selection of which are shown here.

The covers shown do not represent all the versions produced by Haynes, as the manual was revised regularly with supplements to cover each revision of the Fizzy as it appeared.

simple hobby can escalate into an obsession!

Essential documents

This book is intended to provide an insight into the problems encountered when restoring an FS1-E, and to give tips and advice gained by the author's experience and mistakes. A restorer

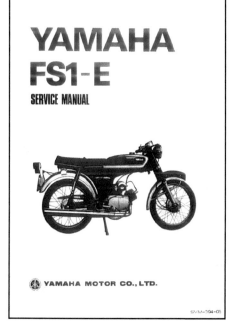

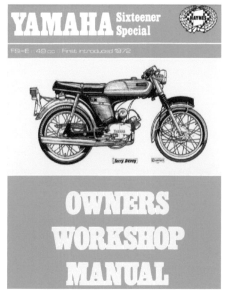

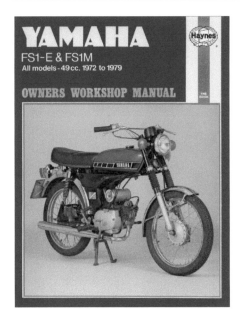

USING THIS BOOK

The author, editors, publisher and retailer cannot accept any responsibility for personal injury, mechanical damage, or financial loss which results from errors or omission in the information given. If this disclaimer is not acceptable to you, please immediately return your unused pristine book and receipt to your retailer who will refund the purchase price paid.

Safety! – During work of any type on your FS1-E, your personal safety MUST always be your prime consideration. You must not undertake any of the work described in this book yourself unless you have sufficient experience, aptitude and workshop facilities and equipment to ensure your personal safety at ALL times.

As stated in the Introduction, the primary purpose of this book is to guide the reader through the selection, purchase, repair and home restoration of an FS1-E. The book is not intended to be a workshop manual, operations or spares manual, but it is meant to supplement and complement these invaluable sources of information. Consequently, you would be well advised to purchase the manual(s) relevant to your particular model before embarking upon a significant repair, and certainly before starting a complete restoration.

References to 'right side' and 'left side' are from the point of view of sitting on the FS1-E looking forward.

www.velocebooks.com / www.veloce.co.uk
Details of all current books • New book news • Special offers • Gift vouchers • Forum

Dedication & acknowledgements

DEDICATION

This book is dedicated to a number of people. Firstly, my wife, Susie, who has not only been totally understanding about the time I have spent on this project, but has travelled all over the country with me collecting rusty wrecks and parts, and has spent hours in breakers' yards sorting through boxes of junk (but she can now tell FS1-E parts from those of other machines). She has also driven alone from Surrey to Liverpool and back in a day to collect one particular wreck!

This book is also dedicated to my children, Jack, Amy, Charlotte, Danielle and James, for all their efforts, but especially to my 12-year-old daughter Amy, who has stripped at least three machines!

Finally, this book is dedicated to my parents who allowed me, against their better judgement, to buy my first FS1-E in 1977.

I'd like to thank Rod Grainger of Veloce Publishing (purchaser of an FS1-E for one of his teenage sons), for asking me to take on this project and having the faith and patience to see it through, and all the FS1-E owners I've met, for their advice and tips during my restorations and, in particular, Nigel Thorne.

ACKNOWLEDGEMENTS

I've had a great deal of support and assistance with this project but I would particularly like to mention the following people: Andrew Smith, Managing Director of Yamaha UK and ex-FS1-E owner, for his assistance with facts, figures and various documents; Penny Cox, Motorcycle Editorial Manager at Haynes Publishing and an ex-FS1-E owner, for her interest in this project and the archive of Haynes manual covers; Paul Davies of Paul's Bodyshop, ex-FS1-E owner, for his painstaking efforts in colour matching; Phil Corsi of Sussex Signs, also an ex-FS1-E owner, for reproducing the decals; Pat Patel of Motomax (yep, an ex-FS1-E owner) for locating all my spare parts; and Mick Lewis for all his assistance with solving my various computer dramas.

Chapter 1
What to restore?

1975 FS1-E - UNRESTORED

The model shown in this section is a 1975 drum brake type. This machine would be a good choice for restoration, should you be lucky enough to find one, as it's generally complete. Although at first glance it looks quite sound, it does need total restoration, though it hasn't suffered from too much abuse during its early years. Apart from alterations to the original paintwork and a lack of indicators it's all there! On closer examination I found that the machine had a number of areas which were damaged and needed attention.

The pictures on the following pages show close-ups of each area of concern, together with an explanation of the damage and advice on how to carry out the repairs.

Right- and left-hand views of an unrestored 1975 FS1-E in Popsicle Purple.

The front fork lower outer tubes have been painted black. The tubes are in generally good condition; they can sometimes be bent where the wheel spindle goes through. The brake plate is on the right-hand side, which is correct for this model. Later versions had the brake plate on the left and the lower tubes have totally different spindle brackets and are not interchangeable. The chrome fork collars at the top of the lower tube are fairly rusty and pitted. The collars are still available, but expensive, and can be re-chromed more cheaply than replaced.

The front mudguard shows signs of accident damage, i.e. it is buckled at the front, and also has surface rust. This mudguard is taken from an earlier machine; this is apparent from the holes you can see that have been drilled for the earlier 'bacon slicer' numberplate. Additionally, later models with left-hand side brakes had the rubber cushion on the left, earlier models were on the right. This mudguard will definitely have to be replaced, probably by sourcing from a breaker, or by using a good pattern replacement (a replica part).

The headlight shrouds are damaged by rust and scratches. There are many available second-hand, but they can be repaired providing the metal is not cracked. The shrouds and the headlamp have at some time been painted black, and there are signs of rust. On this age model they should be body-coloured. Also, the indicators are missing. The chrome collars at the base of the shrouds are fairly rusted. Again, these can be replaced, although often can be polished if not too pitted. So, if it's replacement you need, it's a trip to the breaker or the autojumble.

Another view of the incorrectly painted headlamp shell.

In this photograph you can tell that the washers at the top of the fork leg are not original, as they're far too big. Replacements can be sourced from your local Yamaha dealer. Also, note the rust on the headlamp shell.

The photographs above and right show in detail the right and left handlebar switches. The right-hand switch is in very poor condition. The thread for the wing mirror has been damaged and has a section missing, and the upper casing is cracked. Although this switch is no longer serviceable, don't discard it as it's worth keeping for the lower section, the internals, and the switch button. Always remember that, when restoring your model, never throw anything away – you may be able to use it later, or even trade it with another enthusiast!

The left-hand switch has similar damage. The mirror socket has also been damaged and the choke cable socket has been broken off. Both have been repaired with glue. The choke lever is surprisingly complete, which is rare. Also, the choke lever screw has been replaced with a non-standard part.

Seats in good condition are very hard to find, though the seat shown here has a good pan and the foam has not perished as is common in machines of this age. It has been re-covered quite badly, though, using a patterned seat cover which is not the same design as the original. Note that the original chrome trim has been replaced with black rubber trim.

Rear mudguards are very susceptible to corrosion and damage. Both sides of this one are cracked. It can be seen from the photographs that attempts have been made to repair the broken bracket on the rear mudguard, by screwing an additional bracket on top of the original. This is a look that would definitely not feature on a true restoration.

If the guard is generally solid or has just minor damage, it would be worth considering repairing and rechroming. The tunnel on the section behind the seat was only fitted to early FS1-Es and most replacements don't have this. Additionally, pattern guards have all the wrong tail light mounting holes. Consequently, good used mudguards can be costly and are rare.

This photograph shows heavy rust at the bottom of the frame, and an incorrect mudguard bolt.

Chain guards and pedal guards have very often been altered from the original specification. Both the chain and pedal guards would originally have been silver. Many machines were fitted with extra chrome – chain guards, pedal guards, air box, side panels, headlamp shells and shrouds. If chrome parts have been fitted they would be pattern parts and not genuine Yamaha.

Exhaust pipes rarely last well. Being a two stroke machine, it's unlikely that the exhaust will have rusted inside. Problems will most likely be external rust, general scratches and dents (particularly where the kickstart pedal passes the silencer). In many cases, the original pipe would have been replaced by an aftermarket expansion chamber. This particular pipe is rusty, which is presumably why the chrome has been painted over.

Unusually for an old model this machine does have the correct shock absorbers fitted. Early models have the enclosed spring, whereas later models have the open spring.

Young owners would often attempt to make their machine appear newer by replacing the shocks with later ones. The enclosed shocks were only sold as complete sealed units, so chrome lower sections or painted upper sections weren't available separately. When restoring your FS1-E you will quite often find that the chrome sections will be badly rusted. Refer to the suspension section of this book for details of refurbishing.

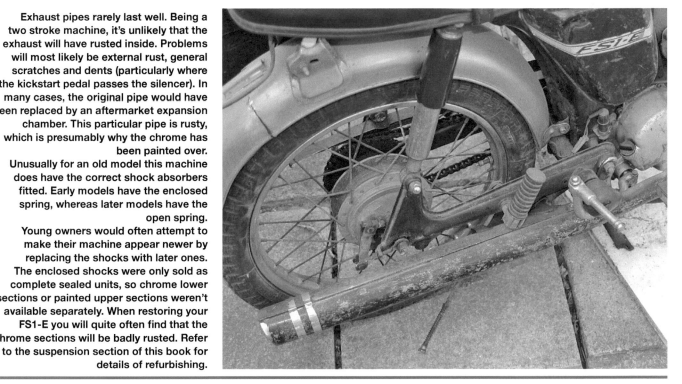

The kickstart lever and the kickstart shaft are connected by matching splines. If the bolt holding the lever to the shaft is not tight, or the lever has been fitted incorrectly, the splines on either the lever, the shaft, or both, will start to wear, and ultimately the pedal will just spin on the shaft. This is what has happened to this machine. The previous owner has actually welded the two together. Firstly, both pedal and shaft are now scrap, and secondly, to carry out any engine repairs the kickstart mechanism would have to be cut off anyway. Thirdly, it appears that a new lever has been used and welded on – these pedals are not readily available.

FS1-Es were only fitted with a centre stand which, surprisingly, often suffers badly from wear. The feet wear off the base, and the stands can bend, causing the pivot point in the frame to become worn (the machine will then not sit on the stand). This is all due to the fact that riders would sit on the bike with the stand down.

1975 FS1-E, BOUGHT AS RESTORED

If, after reading the foregoing, you feel that you don't want to take on a full restoration of an original, unrestored wreck, which can be a very time-consuming project, an alternative would be to purchase a restored machine. This may seem like a good choice, if you can afford it, but be careful! The machine shown here was bought as a fully restored FS1-E, but it did, in fact, start life as an FS1-ED, an early DX model. The prefix on the frame is 596, which designates the DX model, whereas the engine prefix is 394, which designates a drum brake model. The machine has clearly been restored, but it is an amalgamation of many different parts. Therefore, it's important that you check that you're actually getting an original model, before you part with your cash.

With a machine such as this 'restored' model, the restorer must decide whether to rebuild correctly as a DX, requiring sourcing a complete front end, wiring loom and ignition switch, etc., or simply tidy up the machine and keep it as a drum brake model. My advice, in this case, would be the first option. There's a large network of other restorers around who will trade parts, and it's very likely that someone else would have the parts you want, and vice versa.

The 'restored' machine would cost two or three times more than the unrestored version to buy, but the final cost of restoring either machine would average out the same. The full restoration is a longer project and a much dirtier job, so the choice rests with the 'would be' restorer.

Right- and left-hand views of a 'restored' 1975 FS1-E (or is it an FS1-E DX?) finished in Baja Brown.

The front forks on this machine are taken from an FS1-E, but the gaiters are from a DX. The DX gaiters have a larger diameter and, as a result, don't fit firmly over the fork collars. The fork collars should be chrome. These have been partially painted, presumably at the same time as the lower fork tubes.

This seat looks good and in perfect condition, but it's not original. This type of seat, known as a 'buddy seat', was often fitted during the early life of FS1-Es. It was a cheap replacement for a damaged original but did rather change the bike's appearance.

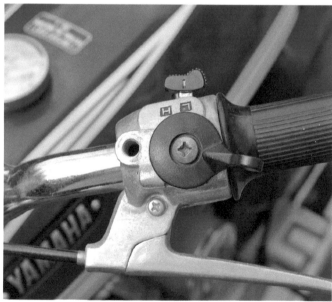

The left-hand handle bar switch, again for an FS1-E, has been fitted with a plastic, pattern, choke lever. The genuine lever would have been alloy. This choke lever is not even connected as the later pull choke carburettor has been fitted. A close-up of this type of carburettor is shown in the following photograph.

This Drum Brake FS1-E should have a cable choke, not the later pull type.

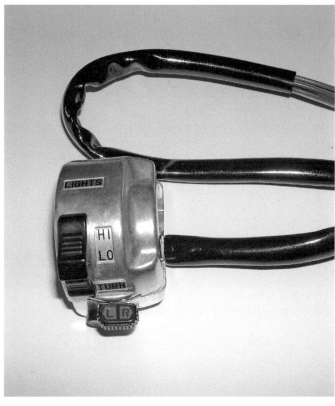

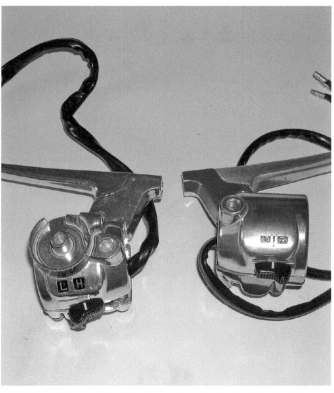

The DX model had a completely different switch arrangement, with all the controls on the left-hand switch.

FS1-E switchgear. The FS1-E was fitted with the high/low beam switch and horn on the left, and indicator switch on the right. The DX had all switches on the left.

Both the early FS1-E and FS1-E DX were mopeds and were equipped with a fully functional pedal system. The pedal system has been totally removed from this machine and a footrest bar fitted. This was often carried out by owners who had become 17-years-old and were able to take their motorcycle test, and then wanted to make their machines look more like 'proper' motorbikes.

Although the pedal chainguard is fitted and correctly finished in silver, the drive chainguard is an aftermarket chrome version.

The right side view of the machine again shows the footrest bar. The kickstart lever is from a much later FS1 model, which wasn't fitted with pedals. The bracket for the rear brake light switch appears to be home-made. Also, the crankcase screws have been replaced with Allen screws. Although this is not standard, it is an advantage when stripping the engine, but the originals were crosshead screws.

As was the case with the unrestored model shown earlier, the rear mudguard is buckled and cracked. The tail light bracket stay is fitted, these have become rather scarce, though this example is fitted with the wrong bolts.

Which option would you choose?

CAN ANY FS1-E BE RESTORED?

In almost all instances, any wrecked and neglected FS1-E can be restored. The 1974 model shown in the accompanying photograph is in extremely poor condition. It is very rusty, the engine has seized and the forks and bottom yolk are bent and also show signs of major rust.

Once the machine was stripped down I discovered major problems, in particular extensive rust damage to the frame where some areas have completely rusted away.

What a mess! But this one can be restored.

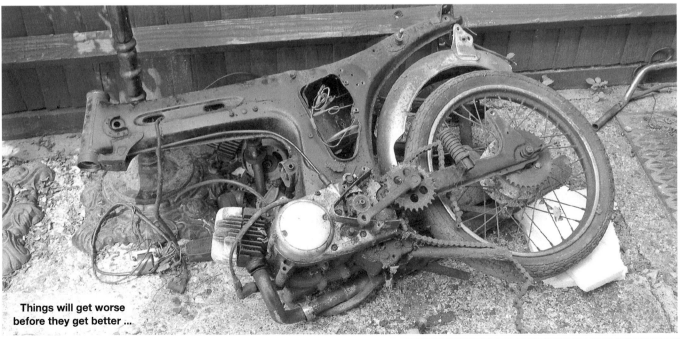

Things will get worse before they get better ...

Many FS1-Es have been neglected for decades.

This is a 1975 early FS1-E DX, known as an FS1-ED. It arrived as a pile of bits and pieces, many of which were unrelated to this particular model. The forks were missing, the tank and tail lights were wrong, and the swinging arm came from a non-pedal type. Taking on a restoration such as this is definitely not for the novice restorer.

Above and opposite top: Even though this example may look as if there's too much to take on, it is, in fact, an ideal project bike. From an initial look it clearly has the correct front end complete with the right-hand side brake plate and, although it has been very neglected, it's nearly all there.

While conducting my extensive searches for potential restorations I have discovered, and in fact purchased, a number of challenging projects. In some instances, potential restorations turn up as boxes of bits, which are almost always advertised as 'complete'. Unless you're very familiar with the construction of and the parts used in putting together an FS1-E, be very careful when approaching such a restoration, as nearly all components vary between models, even the frames!

If it's cheap enough, go for it, but be aware that something described as 'complete' invariably isn't!

This is an odd one! This 1973 FS1-E has an autolube pump. The conversion had been carried out well. Included with the bike was a side panel from a Yamaha YB100 which was a two stroke tank. A dual pull throttle cable had also been fitted.

The back end is a bit of a mess. The shock absorbers and the rear mudguard are from a much later model. As always, the seat is in very poor condition.

The handlebars are from a DX model, as is the top-mounted ignition switch. The handlebar clamps, shell and shrouds have been painted black. It's obvious that, at some stage, an owner has attempted to make this look like a later model.

It's very unlikely that any machine in this sort of condition will have serviceable tyres. This one is beyond use. However, it does demonstrate the wrong type of tyre for an FS1-E front wheel. The original and recommended fitment is a ribbed tyre.

Studying the above photographs you will see that, once again, both handlebar switches are damaged beyond repair, and the levers are without their ball ends.

The tail light assembly is without the support brace and the lens is smashed but the main bracket, under the rust, is in good condition and not cracked.

The left-hand side panel is missing, as is the ignition switch and air box end caps.

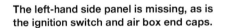

Overall, this example is in poor condition but is definitely worth restoring. The general look of this FS1-E should enable the restorer to pick up a bargain. Had this bike had less rust and less damage it would have looked much more presentable, but the slightly better chrome and shiny parts will still be replaced by the restorer, so another tip is to always look beyond the rust.

HISTORY

The FS1-E heyday was a period between 1972 to 1978 when the restricted models were introduced.

Year	UK sales
1973-1974	11,816
1974-1975	19,841
1975-1976	15,995
1976-1977	11,420
1977-1978	8597
1978-1979	4032
1979-1980	1143
1980-1981	452

The last year that unrestricted models were available to buy was 1977, models registered after 1 August that year were the FS1 model, sales then quickly fell, which resulted in higher prices for used, pre-August 1977 machines.

It seems that, generally, due to nostalgia, most would-be restorers

Don't be put off if lots of parts are missing, this one has the correct major components and the engine and frame numbers match. It even has a V5!

This is a complete 'bitsa' and only worth having for spares as it has no real identity as a particular model.

Although it has a late front end, this example is an ideal restoration project. As it's virtually complete, restoring it will generally be just a cosmetic job.

Year	Prefix	Colour
1973	394	Candy Gold
1974	394	Candy Gold and Popsicle Purple (R1)
1975	394	Popsicle Purple (R9) and Baja Brown
1975	596	Competition Yellow
1976	394	Baja Brown
1976	596	Competition Yellow
1977	394	Baja Brown-Speedblock
1977	596	Competition Yellow-Speedblock

FS1-E colours and colour codes.

choose to restore an identical machine to the one they owned as a sixteen-year-old, or the one they wanted but were not allowed to have. As a rule, it's more lucrative to restore an early pedal model, though the result of their popularity causes a scarcity of spares and machines to restore which leads to these items becoming far more expensive and difficult to source.

Later models appear to be far less popular, machines and spares are much easier to obtain, and cost far less. When restored and complete they are worth nowhere near the value of a sympathetically and properly restored earlier model.

A lot of emphasis is placed on machine frame and engine numbers matching. Whilst it is not essential, or always possible, it is preferable and can reduce the value of a machine should they not match. Unfortunately, as the engines are very easy to swap, when the original engine required major work, many engines were exchanged and the original thrown away.

Some purists argue that a proper restoration should be carried out with all genuine parts. Again, this is not always possible or is costly. Surely it is better to complete a restoration and ride it than to wait for a genuine part to turn up or pay the extortionate prices that some people charge for original parts.

www.velocebooks.com / www.veloce.co.uk
Details of all current books • New book news • Special offers • Gift vouchers • Forum

29

Chapter 2
Preparation

Before starting to strip the bike you should thoroughly clean and degrease everything. Using a cleaning agent, such as Gunk or Jizer, brush the whole bike with the cleaning agent, working particularly around the engine, rear wheel, and, after removing the left-hand engine casing, all around the engine drive sprocket. Hose or jet wash until clean. It will be necessary to repeat this process several times, but it's definitely worth spending time on this as the strip down will become a far easier process.

After the bike is dry, liberally spray all nuts and bolts with WD40 or some other penetrating fluid. Again, repeat this process several times to allow the fluid to penetrate as much as possible.

TOOLS

Bear in mind that your machine could be over thirty years old and many components will have been untouched since its manufacture and, as they were only intended to have a fairly short life, many components will be weak and in poor condition.

The machine will require generally simple tools for the strip down, and the following list below should contain all that you require to complete the job:

- Impact driver
- Metric socket set
- Metric open and ring spanners
- Socket extension bar
- Angle grinder
- Mole grips
- Mini drill, Dremel or similar
- Blow torch
- Bench grinder and polishing mops
- Sand-blast cabinet (this could be out-sourced)
- Parts washer
- Circlip pliers
- Hacksaw

PARTS

When stripping your machine, as I stressed in chapter 1, never throw anything away. Keep all the parts you remove, however poor their condition, record all removed parts, then bag up or label everything.

If restoring more than one machine, or if you're accumulating spares, it's advisable to prepare an inventory (see the accompanying example).

Another aid to restoration is to obtain a copy of the parts manual. These are readily available and contain exploded diagrams of every part, nut, bolt, and washer. A further restoration aid is a workshop manual, Haynes or similar. These are essential, but are written in an ideal world where the machine being worked on is in good condition to start with and they make no allowances for the ravages of time, neglect, and, worst of all, work carried out by highly unskilled 16-year-old mechanics! Additionally, many machines will have suffered from 'customisers' and budget repairs carried out using parts from different models. One common alteration is that a totally incorrect front end is fitted following an accident.

STRIPDOWN

The general strip down is a fairly basic process.

The seat is fixed to the frame by two nuts at the rear of the frame and two bolts between the seat and the side panels. Remove the nuts and the bolts and lift the seat from the frame.

With the seat removed, the petrol

Description	Part Number	New (tick)	Used (tick)	Colour	Quantity
HANDLE BAR HOLDERS	122-23441-00		✓	METAL	2
FS1E FORK OIL SEALS	1091-23145-01		✓	METAL/RUBBER	2
" DX FORK OIL SEALS	315-23145-00		✓	RUBBER	2
RECTIFIER PLATE	220-81975-00	✓ (re finished)		METAL	2
WIRING HARNESS FS1E	394-82590-20		✓✓ REVIS	WIRE	1
STEERING HEAD BALL RACE	156-23411-00		✓	METAL	3
STEERING/FORK BOLTS	122-23346-01		✓	"	2
BRAKE SHOES	296-25370-00		✓	"	6
" " SPRINGS	90506-16034		✓	"	3
RIGHT LEVER ASSY	109-82820-11-94		✓	"	2
LEFT LEVER	137-83912-01		✓	"	1
RIGHT LEVER	137-83922-01		✓	"	1
" " UPPER HOLDER	109-82820-11-94		✓	"	1
IGNITION COIL	355-82310-40		✓	"	2
260-83510-31					
SPEEDOMETER ASSY	260-83510-31		✓	"	3
SOCKET ASSY (SPEEDO LEADS)	260-83520-11		✓	WIRES	2
HEADLAMP SOCKET CORD ASSY	241-84312-00		✓	"	3
TAIL LAMP UNIT ASSY	120-84510-32	✓		METAL/PLASTIC	1
FRONT BRAKE CABLE ADJUSTER	90123-06011	✓		METAL	4
FS1E-DX WIRE HOLDER (FRONT MUDGUARD)	174-21518-00			CHROME	1
H/LAMP LENS RETAINING CLIPS	195-84324-00	✓		METAL	3
SILENCER DAMPER	237-83523-00	✓ (2)	✓ (1)	RUBBER	3
COTTER PIN (PEDALS)	210-27813-00	✓		METAL	2
HANDLEBAR BOLT	91214-06035		✓	"	7
" WASHER	92901-06600		✓	"	3
FORK CAP WASHER	207-23112-00	✓ (2) REV Fork	✓ (3)	"	5
FORK CAP BOLT	260-23311-40		✓	"	1
STEERING HEAD BOLT	122-23451-00		✓	"	2
LHS HANDLE SWITCH	393-83973-01		✓	"	2
FS1E-DX LEVER ASSY (RIGHT)			✓		1
KNEE RIGHT SIDE COVER	209-21724-00	✓ (3)	✓ (1)	METAL	3
COLLAR (FRONT WHEEL SPACER)	128-25183-00		✓	"	2
FS1E THROTTLE (TUBE)	137-26243-60		✓	METAL + PLASTIC	3
" " CABLE	394-26311-70		✓	" "	1
" " GRIP	137-26242-60		✓	RUBBER	1
FS1E DX THROTTLE CABLE	596-26311-20		✓	Metal + Plastic	1
FS1E-DX LHS COVER KNOB	122-21724-00	✓ (2)	✓ (2)	" "	4
FS1E KNOB SIDE COVER LEFT	102-21714-00		✓	PLASTIC	1
FS1E FLASHER RELAY		✓		METAL	1
FS1E-DX IGNITION SWITCH — PARTS (See also complete 1)			✓		1
FS1E STEERING LOCK PARTS			✓	METAL	2
FS1E PLATE (FRONT HUB)	109-25121-01-35	SLIGHT DAMAGE ✓		"	1
DX HOUSING GEARUNIT (SPEEDO)	390-25194-00		✓	"	1
DX FRONT FORK CROWN	185-23435-00-78		✓	"	1
" HANDLEBAR HOLDERS	466-23442-00 + 122-23941-00		✓	ALU	2 + 2
" SPEEDO BRACKET	—		✓	METAL	1
FS1E FRONT BRAKE CABLE	260-26341-10		✓	WIRE	1
" " " "	109-26341-20	(Short)	✓	WIRE	1
DX SPEEDO CABLE	481-83550-00		✓	"	1
CLUTCH CABLE	283-26335-00		✓	"	2
THROTTLE CABLE FS1E	394-26311-10		✓	"	2

Parts inventory.

tank can now be removed. Turn the fuel tap to the off position, remove the rubber petrol feed pipe, then attach a section of fuel pipe to the tank, place the open end into a suitable petrol can, and drain any remaining petrol.

Pull the fuel tank gently towards the rear of the frame and, at the same time, lift the rear of the tank – the tank will now clear the frame. Remove all the rubber dampers from the tank and store them for re-use. Remove the fuel tap from the tank and store this for refurbishment.

Remove the side panels by unscrewing the knobs.

During the pre-strip down cleaning process, the left-hand engine casing will have been removed, giving access to all the engine mounting bolts. After removing the drive chain, using the split link, slacken all the engine mounting bolts and remove the engine. Refer to a workshop manual for full details of this process.

The machine will now be much lighter and easier to work on.

The remaining process of the strip down is simply a case of removing all the components, though there are a number of areas that are likely to be difficult. I have listed solutions to the problems you are likely to encounter in the following sections.

Pedal shaft

The pedal shaft is the steel shaft that passes through the swinging arm. This was rarely used and, as a result, is almost always seized. The pedal cranks are secured by cotter pins and circlips. After removing these, it may be necessary to heat the cranks with a blowtorch to remove them. With the shaft exposed, lay the machine on its right-hand side and apply penetrating oil. When this has had a chance to do its work, lightly tap the left end of the shaft. This may be enough to move the shaft, but more effort is usually required. Using a club hammer, tap the left-hand end of the shaft, at the same time applying heat with a blowtorch to the outer shaft on the swing arm. With enough encouragement

The drive chain damper must be fitted before installing the swinging arm.

The pedal shaft must be greased before being installed.

the shaft will start to move. The process of tapping the end of the shaft will have resulted in the end of the shaft splaying over, and this will not go through the tight fit of the outer swing arm shaft. Using a Dremel type drill, with a grinding bit, the tip of the shaft can be ground sufficiently to allow the shaft to pass through. The remainder of the shaft

can be tapped out using a long bolt or similar.

The same process can be applied to the swinging arm pivot bolt, as shown in the accompanying photograph.

With all components removed from the frame, it may now be refurbished. Depending on its condition, it can be sand-blasted and coated, along with

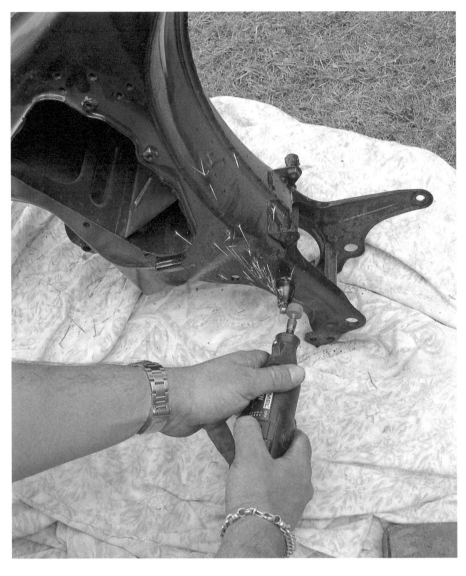

the operation becomes quite easy.

Place the lower mounting lug in a vice, or insert a screwdriver, grip the lower chrome section of the shock absorber and pull upwards. This action will expose a nut with two flat sides. Using a 17mm open spanner, slacken the nut and then slowly turn the upper section of the shock absorber. The spindle inside the casing will now unscrew from the lower lug and will become detached. Withdraw the lower cover and the spring. Next, pull the upper cover down as far as possible and then return this to the top. This action will reveal a plastic flanged washer, which can now be removed over the rubber damper at the base of the spindle. The upper cover can now be removed.

The lower cover, depending on the condition, may be refurbished by polishing or re-chroming. Typically, though, these are in poor condition and are unserviceable. As previously stated, the shock absorbers were only supplied as complete units and no spare parts are available, though the lower sections from the Honda C50, C70, etc., make an ideal replacement and are readily available in breakers' yards at a fraction of FS1-E prices. The Honda unit is dismantled in the same way as the Yamaha, except that the lock nut is 19mm. The lower sections are slightly longer, but as they're

the swing arm, yokes and stand, or, if it's very rusty, it would be preferable to sand-blast it and have all the pitting filled and then sprayed.

At this stage all the bodywork will be available for painting except the shock absorber tops.

Shock absorbers

The rear shock absorbers on the early pedal FS1-E are fully enclosed, with chrome lower sections and body-coloured top sections. The units were only supplied as complete sealed units, and no parts were available separately. They are now discontinued parts, and very few new old stock parts

An unrestored FS1-E shock absorber.

are available, and those that are are very expensive and invariably have the incorrect lower mounting bracket. Therefore, in most cases, refurbishment of the parts is the only option.

The shock absorbers can be dismantled and, once you've done one,

covered by the top cover, this is not a problem. The hole in the base is also larger, so it's advisable to use the Honda nut when reassembling, to prevent the cover becoming misaligned.

The FS1-E upper cover may be treated as the rest of the bodywork and

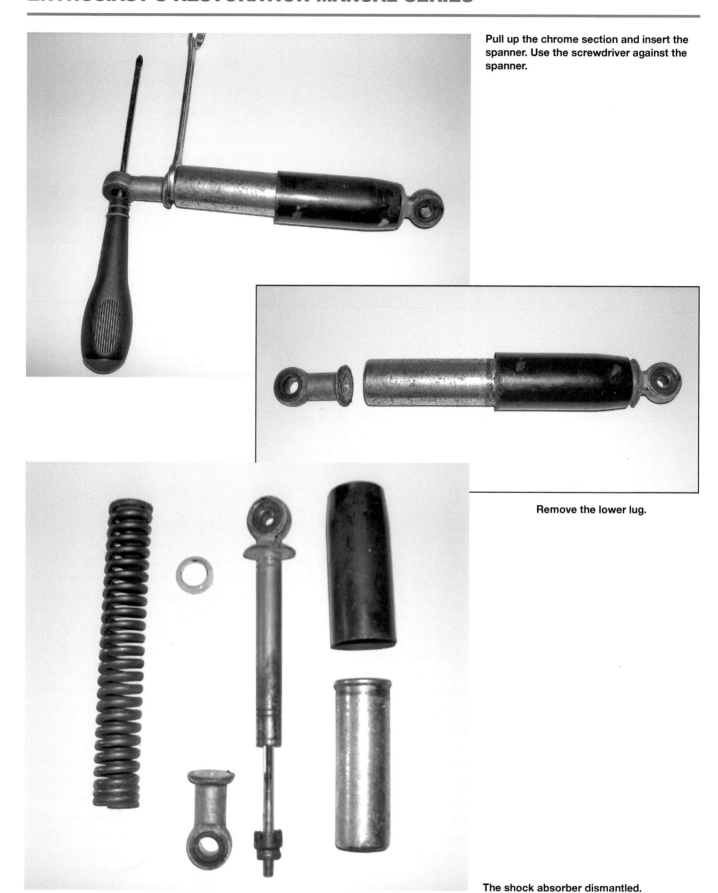

Pull up the chrome section and insert the spanner. Use the screwdriver against the spanner.

Remove the lower lug.

The shock absorber dismantled.

The shock absorber reassembled with replacement chrome section and repainted top.

This 1974 model has been fitted with later shock absorbers – some time ago judging by the condition.

This 1975 model has its original shock absorbers but condition is poor.

repainted. The Honda top covers will fit, but aren't the same shape, with straight sides as opposed to the taper of the FS1-E.

The top and bottom fixing lugs are aluminium and were originally lacquered. These can be easily refurbished. Firstly, remove the lacquer with paint stripper. Using a bench grinder with a polishing mop, the main areas can quickly be repolished, the awkward areas can be polished using a Dremel type drill with a polishing head. To obtain the original brushed finish, a Scotch pad can be used in sweeping motions to obtain the correct line direction.

Finally, re-lacquer both lugs.

Reassembly is the reverse of dismantling, but it's advisable to insert cardboard between the lower lug and chrome section to avoid damage.

The same process can be used on the exposed spring type shock absorbers to enable the springs to be removed for re-chroming, but the lock nut is 19mm and not 17mm.

Swinging arm

The swinging arm has a number of problem areas. The removal of the pedal gear has previously been described, and it is definitely advisable to carry out this operation before removing the swinging arm from the frame, to give better purchase when tapping out the shaft.

Removing the swing arm bolt is by the same process as the pedal shaft, but any tapping directly on to the bolt will damage the thread. By installing nuts onto the bolt prior to tapping it, and gradually removing them as the bolt moves, it may be possible to salvage the bolt, but it many cases this will have to be replaced.

Wherever possible, the original swing arm should be salvaged. These have become quite rare, and often those advertised for sale are for later models and, whilst they will fit, there are no lugs for the pedal gear. It's possible to modify a later arm but this can be costly.

The swinging arm pivots on two rubber/metal bushes. At first glance

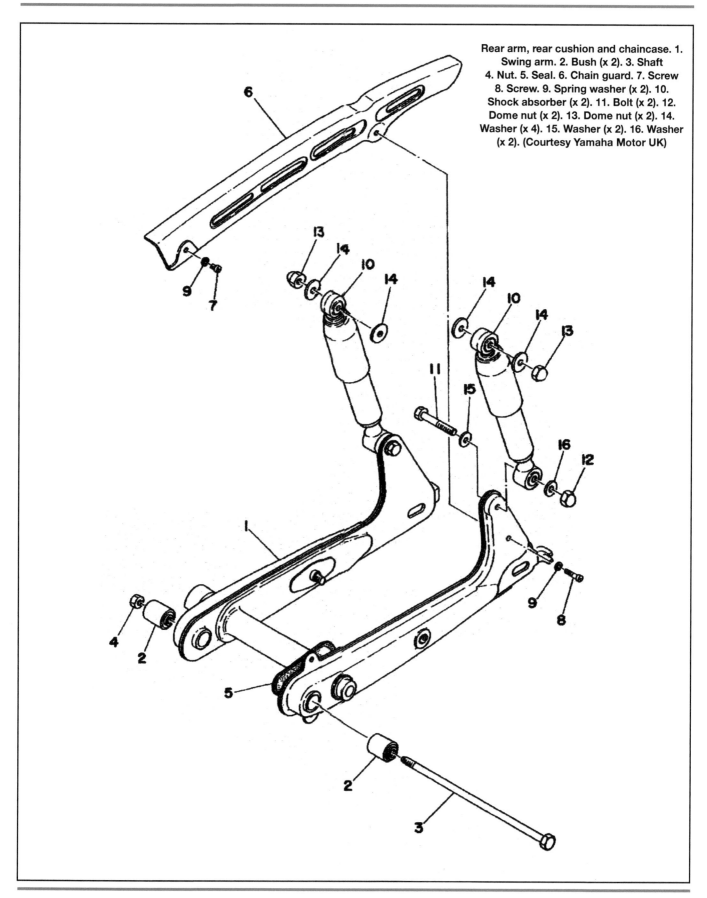

Rear arm, rear cushion and chaincase. 1. Swing arm. 2. Bush (x 2). 3. Shaft 4. Nut. 5. Seal. 6. Chain guard. 7. Screw 8. Screw. 9. Spring washer (x 2). 10. Shock absorber (x 2). 11. Bolt (x 2). 12. Dome nut (x 2). 13. Dome nut (x 2). 14. Washer (x 4). 15. Washer (x 2). 16. Washer (x 2). (Courtesy Yamaha Motor UK)

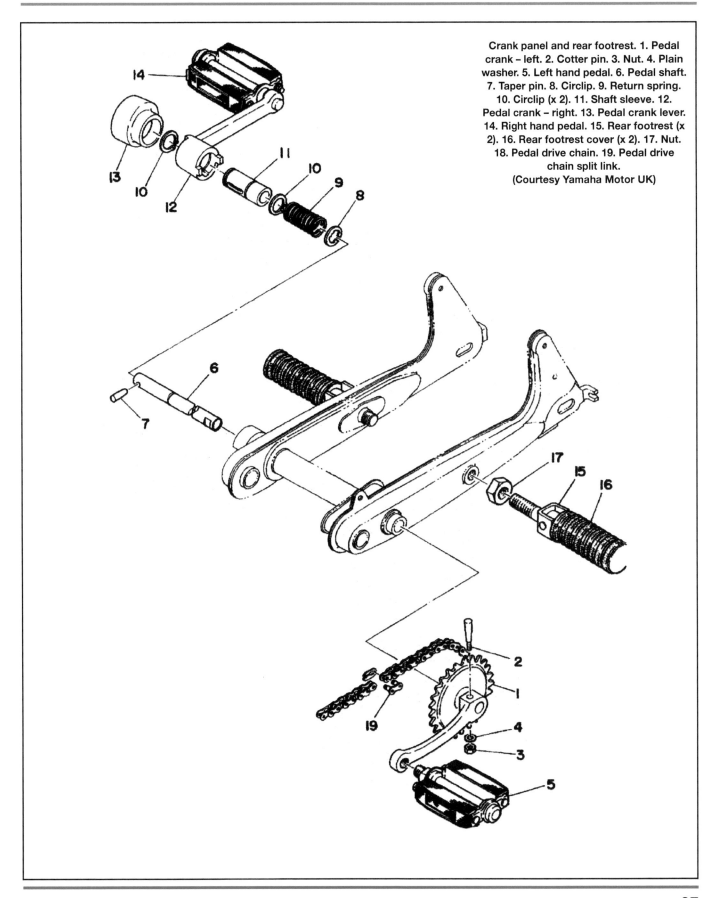

Crank panel and rear footrest. 1. Pedal crank – left. 2. Cotter pin. 3. Nut. 4. Plain washer. 5. Left hand pedal. 6. Pedal shaft. 7. Taper pin. 8. Circlip. 9. Return spring. 10. Circlip (x 2). 11. Shaft sleeve. 12. Pedal crank – right. 13. Pedal crank lever. 14. Right hand pedal. 15. Rear footrest (x 2). 16. Rear footrest cover (x 2). 17. Nut. 18. Pedal drive chain. 19. Pedal drive chain split link.
(Courtesy Yamaha Motor UK)

Swinging arm.

these usually appear to be in good condition, but it would be advisable to replace them as they are still available and not expensive (also, if the arm is to be stove enamelled, the process will melt the rubber).

Removal can be carried out using the various methods explained below.

Method 1

The bushes can be heated using a blowtorch to melt the rubber sufficiently to allow the inner sleeve to be tapped out. By inserting a bolt the same diameter as the pivot bolt and then heating the bush, one tap to the bolt head will usually be enough to knock out the inner sleeve and part of the rubber.

The remaining outer sleeve can again be heated and tapped out.

Method 2

Insert the blade of a junior hacksaw inside the inner sleeve of the bush, then connect the blade to the handle of the hacksaw and saw through the bush in two places. The bush can then be tapped out.

Bush fitting

Once the swinging arm has been refurbished, the new bushes may be installed by drifting them in. This should be carried out using either a rubber hammer or a hammer with wood protecting the bush and swing arm.

To aid this process, liberally coat the swinging bush location with washing up liquid. Another tip is to put the bushes in the freezer for some time prior to installation, as this will contract the metal fractionally and make the process easier.

Before installing the swinging arm ensure that the drive chain damper is fitted.

It's advisable to coat all shafts and spindles with copper-slip grease prior to assembly. There are very few grease nipples on the FS1-E so shafts and spindles, etc., are not easy to access when complete.

Front forks

On an early FS1-E there are two types of front forks: the drum brake type and the disc brake type (DX).

The 1972-1977 FS1-E was fitted with a twin leading shoe front brake, with the brake plate located on the right-hand side of the wheel hub.

The forks comprise a pair of steel lower outer tubes, differing only in that the right-hand leg has a brake plate locating lug. **Note!** – Be careful when buying new old stock lower legs as the brake plate locating lug is located on the left and, more importantly, the front wheel spindle lug is much wider and will not fit on an early machine.

The picture on the page opposite shows the early FS1-E fork leg on the left, with the later leg with the wider lug on the right.

1972-1977 drum brake forks.

Early (left) and late drum brake fork lowers.

The correct bolt arrangement for handlebar brackets and top yoke.

The lower section of the fork leg is connected to the fork inner (stanchion) by a threaded, chromium-plated collar. Above the collar is the rubber fork gaiter which encloses the fork spring. The correct number of rings on the gaiter is nine.

Each fork leg is clamped into the bottom yoke. Again, the FS1-E and FS1-E DX yokes are different, though interchangeable. The fork leg clamp bolts on the FS1-E are angled, whereas the DX bolts face directly to the front of the bike.

Between the top and bottom yoke are the headlamp shrouds, which sit on chrome cups with rubber dampers, and there are further chrome sections covering the bottom yoke. The DX model covers were fitted with captive nuts for orange reflectors, which were not fitted as standard.

After removing the front wheel and mudguard, the fork top bolt and the bottom yoke bolt can be removed. In many instances the bottom yoke clamp bolt will be seized. Apply penetrating oil to the bolt head and in the rear of the yoke, as the thread is accessible from the rear. It may also be necessary to apply heat to the yoke as often the

Drum brake yoke (left), and disc brake yoke.

original bolt will have been replaced. Always try to remove the bolt slowly as they can shear off in the yoke, so use a socket extension bar and apply even pressure. Shearing the bolt in the yoke can make the yoke unserviceable.

The fork oil can only be drained after the legs have been removed from the bike. To drain the oil, remove the bolt at the top of the leg and safely store the

rubber seal, and then invert the leg and drain.

With the leg removed and the oil drained, clamp the lower leg in a vice (protect the leg with rags or wood to prevent any damage). Grip the upper section of the chrome collar, this is covered by the gaiter and, if scratched during this process will not be visible, and unscrew the collar. With the collar

Unrestored shroud and gaiters.

Shroud and gaiter restoration in progress.

removed, the inner tube will pull out of the lower tube. The collar contains the fork oil seal, which should be removed as a matter of course.

The collars in most instances will be in poor condition. Replacements are still available but are expensive. It may be cheaper to have the originals rechromed, especially if you're having a quantity of rechroming carried out, but the finish will be different from the original, which was slightly dull. This is a decision for the restorer.

The lower tubes suffer quite badly from rust, but generally this is only surface rust, and they can easily be refurbished by sand-blasting and painting or powder coating. Before having them refurbished, check that the bottom lugs are straight, as these are susceptible to accident damage but can be heated and straightened prior to refurbishment. Also check the threads at the top of the fork lower, as these can be cross-threaded, so care must be taken on reassembly.

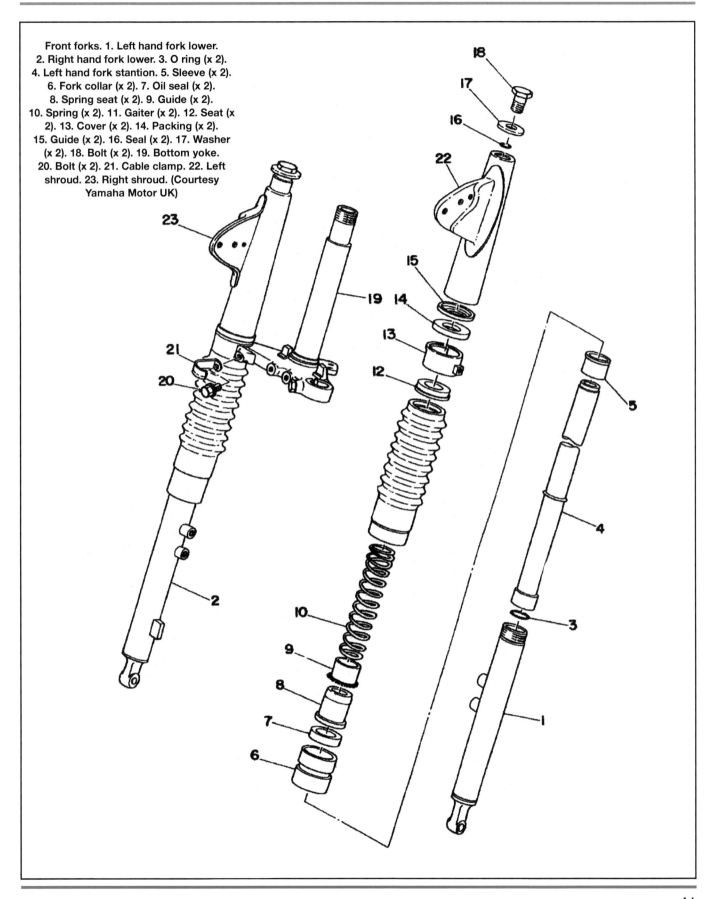

Front forks. 1. Left hand fork lower. 2. Right hand fork lower. 3. O ring (x 2). 4. Left hand fork stantion. 5. Sleeve (x 2). 6. Fork collar (x 2). 7. Oil seal (x 2). 8. Spring seat (x 2). 9. Guide (x 2). 10. Spring (x 2). 11. Gaiter (x 2). 12. Seat (x 2). 13. Cover (x 2). 14. Packing (x 2). 15. Guide (x 2). 16. Seal (x 2). 17. Washer (x 2). 18. Bolt (x 2). 19. Bottom yoke. 20. Bolt (x 2). 21. Cable clamp. 22. Left shroud. 23. Right shroud. (Courtesy Yamaha Motor UK)

FS1-E DX FRONT FORKS

The 1975-1977 FS1-E DX was fitted with an hydraulic front disc brake, with the disc and calliper located on the right-hand side.

The forks comprise a pair of aluminium lower outer tubes and inner stanchions, later disc brake models have different inner and outer tubes and will not fit on an early machine.

The upper section of the DX front fork assembly from the top yoke to the bottom yoke is identical to the drum brake FS1-E, except for the bottom yoke, as previously mentioned. The bottom yoke clamp bolts face the front of the bike, whereas the FS1-E bolts are angled.

The DX has a calliper bolted to the right fork leg, and an hydraulic hose connected to the master cylinder on the handlebars.

Remove the front wheel, including the brake disc, front mudguard, and brake hose. Care should be taken when removing the front mudguard mounting bolts as these can shear off, which will then require the bolts to be drilled out. Slacken the bottom yoke clamp bolt. Refer to the FS1-E fork removal for details of working on the yoke.

The fork legs can be drained by removing drain screws at the side towards the bottom of each leg. Once the majority of the oil has been drained the machine may be pushed forward to force any remaining oil from the legs.

With the oil drained, remove the top yoke by removing the top bolts and oil seal washers. Slacken the bottom yoke clamp bolts and withdraw the legs from the yoke. The gaiter arrangement is the same as the FS1-E, but the gaiters have a larger diameter at the bottom to compensate for the wider leg, and they are not interchangeable between models (again, the number of rings is nine).

To separate the fork lower from the station circlip pliers will be required. Looking into the lower tube from the top, a large circlip will be visible. Pinch the circlip with the pliers and fully remove it. The inner leg should now pull clear

FS1-ED or early FS1-E DX front forks.

Early FS1-ED or DX front brake master cylinder.

from the lower tube and may be fully withdrawn.

The fork oil seal will also pull clear of the lower leg and may be removed. The oil seal should be replaced as a matter of course.

The DX lower tubes were lacquered aluminium. To refurbish the lower tubes, remove the lacquer with paint stripper and thoroughly clean and degrease.

The tubes can be refurbished using a bench grinder with polishing mops. The finish obtained will be high gloss, which was not the original. Using a Scotch

pad, stroke around the leg to achieve a brushed finish. Finally, re-lacquer each leg.

LATER MODELS

After August 1977, the FS1-E and FS1-E DX were no longer available, and the FS1 and FS1 DX models were introduced. Although these machines looked very similar, most of the components are completely different and they are not interchangeable.

The left-hand leg is from an early 1975-1977 DX; the right-hand leg is from a later DX.

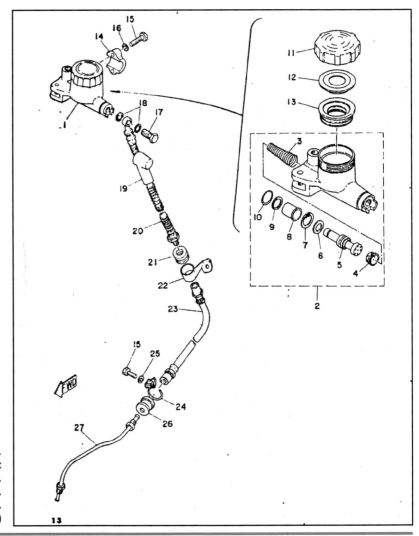

FS1-ED or DX front brake master cylinder. 1. Cap. 2. Diaphragm plate. 3. Diaphragm. 4. Bracket. 5. Bolt (x 3). 6. Spring washer (x 2). 7. Bolt. 8. Washer (x 2). 9. Shroud. 10. Hose. 11. Grommet. 12. Holder. 13. Hose. 14. Holder. 15. Spring washer. 16. Grommet. 17. Brake pipe. (Courtesy Yamaha Motor UK)

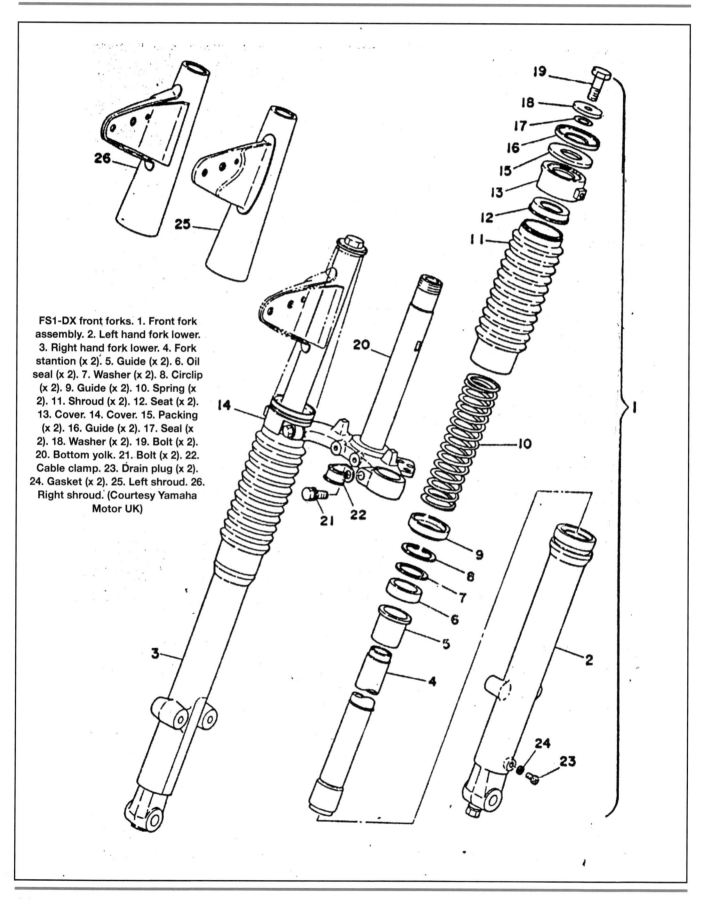

FS1-DX front forks. 1. Front fork assembly. 2. Left hand fork lower. 3. Right hand fork lower. 4. Fork stantion (x 2). 5. Guide (x 2). 6. Oil seal (x 2). 7. Washer (x 2). 8. Circlip (x 2). 9. Guide (x 2). 10. Spring (x 2). 11. Shroud (x 2). 12. Seat (x 2). 13. Cover. 14. Cover. 15. Packing (x 2). 16. Guide (x 2). 17. Seal (x 2). 18. Washer (x 2). 19. Bolt (x 2). 20. Bottom yolk. 21. Bolt (x 2). 22. Cable clamp. 23. Drain plug (x 2). 24. Gasket (x 2). 25. Left shroud. 26. Right shroud. (Courtesy Yamaha Motor UK)

Brake pedal and stand. 1. Centre stand. 2. Shaft. 3. Brake pedal. 4. Circlip. 5. Link. 6. Spring. 7. Bolt. 8. Nut. 9. Brake rod. 10. Washer. 11. Spring. 12. Cotter pin. (Courtesy Yamaha Motor UK)

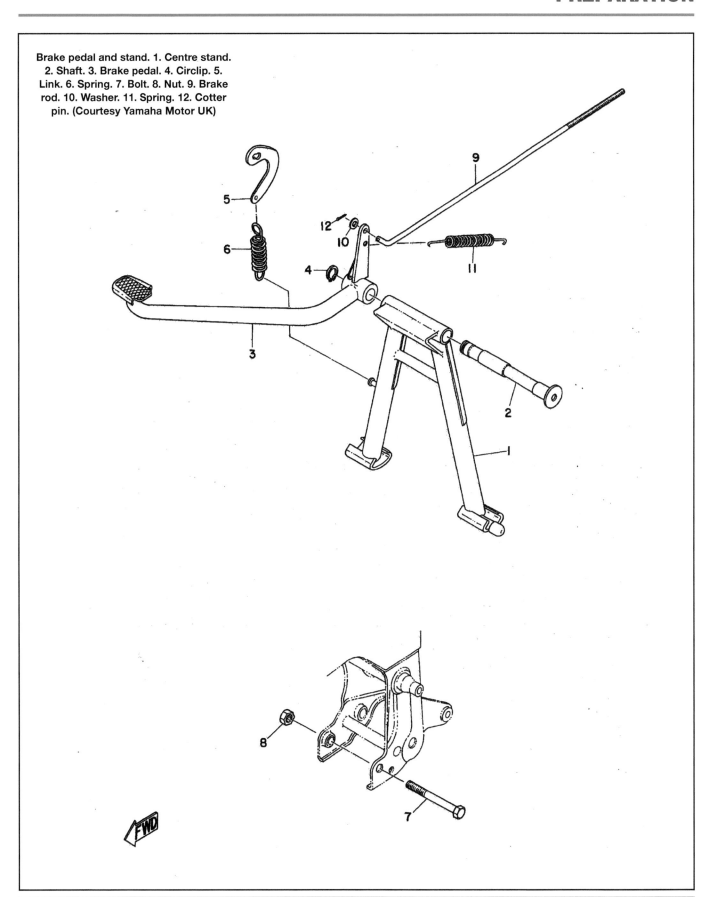

Chapter 3
Chassis

FRAME

The FS1-E and FS1-E DX frames are generally identical. The frame number for an FS1-E has prefix 394, and the DX has prefix 596. The only other difference is that the DX has additional screw holes on the right side of the frame, below the seat, for the helmet lock.

The main problem you'll have when you've sourced your frame is the presence of rust. Many FS1-Es will have spent a great deal of time out doors, neglected and exposed to the elements. One of my finds during this project was a frame half-submerged in a pond at the end of someone's garden!

The model in the accompanying pictures was stored in a shed after the owner had an accident on it which resulted in the bent forks. The shed had disintegrated around the bike and it had not moved since 1978! I think the young owner was forbidden by his parents to use it again, so in the shed it stayed, forgotten. The seat had completely gone, and all that remained of the seat pan were the centre brackets.

One rear seat mounting bracket had rusted away and had to be rebuilt. The poor condition of this frame meant that it could not be powder coated, as all the pitting would have been visible. It was, therefore, necessary to fill all the pitting and have the frame sprayed.

After painting

Before you start refurbishing the frame there are a number of areas which you should check and which can then be remedied.

Check the alignment of the spine down the centre of the frame; this should be straight, but a serious accident could cause this to be misaligned. It's possible to have the frame repaired

FS1-ED frame with helmet lock.

A very neglected FS1-E.

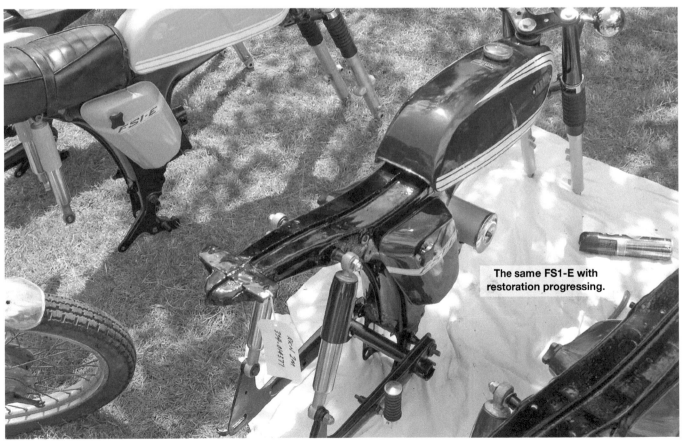

The same FS1-E with restoration progressing.

but if it's too buckled then it would be worth sourcing a replacement. There are complications with this with regard to the frame number, but there are still some new old-stock frames available on eBay which can be stamped with the original number.

Check all threaded holes throughout the entire frame, as it's easier to have these tapped prior to painting.

Check the centre stand mounting lugs at the bottom of the frame. In many instances these circular holes will have become oval-shaped due to the riders sitting on the bike whilst on the stand. A large washer can be welded over the holes inside the frame to create a new round hole.

Check the bottom mudguard mounting points; often these are need of attention. In extreme cases the bracket will be missing, but generally the problem will be with the captive nuts being drilled through.

Before the frame is painted, be sure to mask the shock absorber mounts and the head races contained in the head stock, but also be sure that as much as possible internally is painted, i.e., within the battery compartment.

Apart from serious accident damage, the bottom yolks can nearly always be refurbished. The main problem is shearing off the clamp bolts of the horn fixing bolts. Occasionally, the lock stop lugs on the yolk will have been damaged. Prior to strip down, move the handlebars from lock to lock to determine if the headlamp shrouds make contact with the tank.

Frame restoration

The frame can suffer with general rust problems and, as described earlier, the condition of the frame will dictate whether it can be powder coated or whether it will need filling to repair the pitting, and then painting.

The frame can also suffer damage other than accidental. This frame has had a section roughly cut away, the reason for this cannot be explained, though it can be repaired.

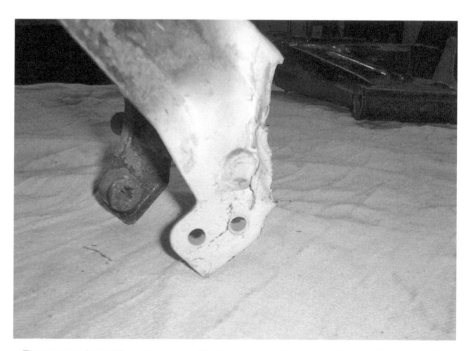

The rear mudguard lower bracket will often have problems, too. In many instances the captive nuts will have been drilled through: this can be remedied by grinding off the nuts and, when refitting the mudguard, using a nut and bolt. This option will detract from the originality of the FS1-E but is the simplest. A better alternative would be to weld new captive nuts onto the bracket.

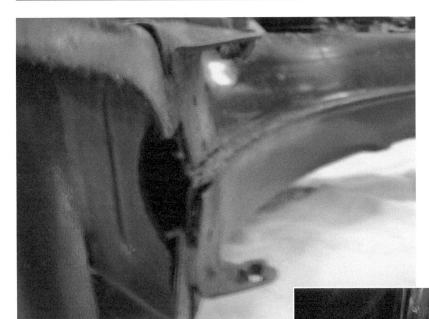

In extreme cases the bracket can be missing. The brackets are quite a simple shape and can be re-made and welded to the frame.

This rear mudguard bracket is missing.

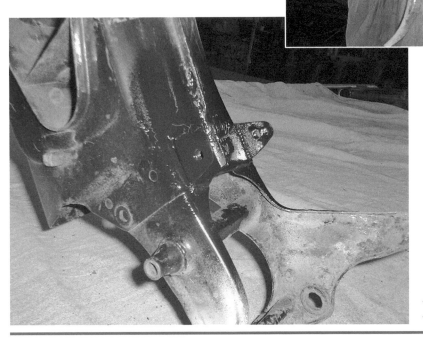

The bracket has been rebuilt and welded onto the frame.

The lower sections of the frame can easily become bent. This frame requires the rear brake arm to be straightened, and the mudguard bracket is missing.

This is how it should look.

The centre stand pivots in the frame will, in many cases, have become oval through wear.
If this is not addressed the stand will flap up and down as the bike is ridden. By welding an appropriate size washer on the inner side of the mounting this problem is easily resolved.

The frame pictured has been fully stripped and is ready for sand-blasting and painting or coating. It still requires the rear brake arm locating bracket to be repaired as this has been cut off.

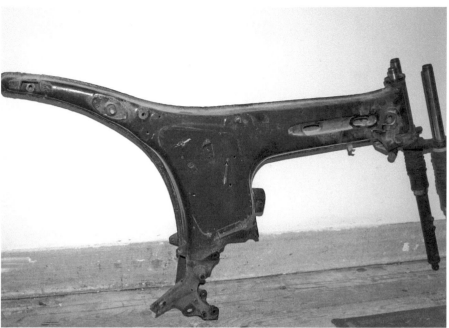

The overall condition of this frame is good (it looks worse than it is). The visible rust is only surface and there are no badly pitted areas. This frame is ideal for stove enamelling as it doesn't necessitate any filling.

It's difficult to see from this picture, but the stove enamelled finish to this frame is perfect.

As the shock absorbers are a tight fit on the mounting lugs, it is advisable to mask the threads. Yamaha paint was much thinner than any new finish and, if these lugs are not masked, the new finish will have to be removed.

It is advisable to loosely fit bolts into threads that are to be used later. Removing new paint from a screw or bolt thread can be difficult and, in extreme cases, require re-tapping.

The head races have been masked prior to recoating. This is worthwhile as removing them can be time-consuming.

New washers were welded into the main stand pivot point on this frame.

The lower bracket for the rear mudguard, including new captive nuts, has been rebuilt on this frame.

SWINGING ARM RESTORATION

Apart from rust, the swinging arm usually requires little attention, but in the example shown in the accompanying pictures the chain guard bracket has been cut off.

There is no reason to have done this, but as replacements for early examples are rare, it's important to attempt to salvage whenever possible.

A steel plate was cut to size, shaped to match the original, and then welded on.

Chain guard bracket removed!

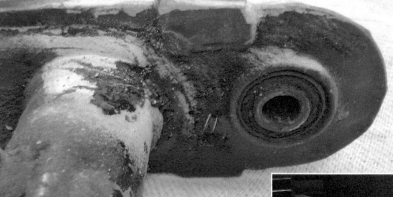

Inner view of the removed chain guard bracket.

The new bracket has been shaped and welded in position.

Inner view of replacement bracket.

Frame side cover. 1. Frame. 2. Engine mounting bolt (x 2). 3. Nut (x 2). 4. Spring (x 2). 5. Left side panel. 6. Side panel knob. 7. Ring. 8. Damper. 9. Damper. 10. Right side panel. 11. Nut. 12. Split pin. 13. Damper. 14. Decal. 15. Tool kit. 16. Decal. 17. Plug. (Courtesy Yamaha Motor UK)

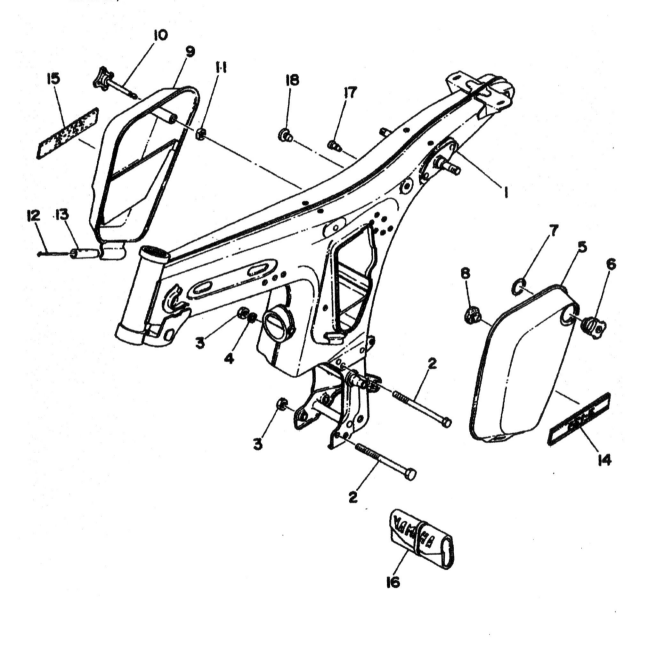

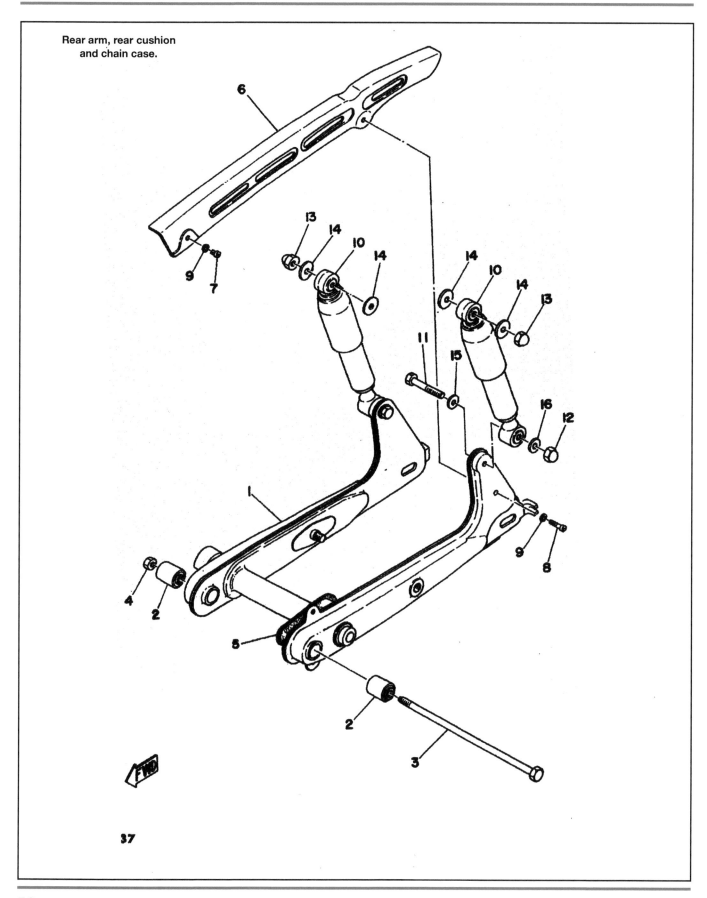

Rear arm, rear cushion
and chain case.

37

Chapter 4
Parts

Apart from the bodywork, FS1-Es have two component colours: black and silver. During the strip down procedure, accumulate all the various coloured parts together, as this will enable you to obtain a better price when you source your paint sprayer.

Black components
- Frame
- Swinging arm
- Centre stand
- Top and bottom yolks
- Speedometer bracket
- Ignition switch bracket (DX only)
- Barrel

Silver components
- Fork legs (FS1-E only)
- Engine casings
- Air box
- Head
- Chain guard
- Pedal chain guard
- Tail light/numberplate bracket

Keep all nuts and bolts and brackets that are serviceable and keep these together, again to get the best price to have all the zinc plating done at the same time.

Zinc components
- Kickstart pedal
- Gear lever
- Rear brake stay
- Rear brake arm
- Rear brake rod
- Front brake arm

Chrome components
- Mudguards
- Air box end caps
- Handlebars
- Speedometer
- Tail light stay

Many components will be in a pretty poor condition, but most can be salvaged and refurbished.

The condition of the right-hand engine casing in the accompanying picture is typical. Many engine casings are repainted in a variety of colours and some are even polished, though the original finish was painted in a dull silver. The casings will require degreasing using Gunk, Jizer or similar. Once this has been thoroughly carried out, the casing can be sand- or bead-blasted. The finished casing has been stove enamelled and the results are excellent. Some small imperfections are still visible, but short of sourcing a new old-stock part, this casing is ideal.

Cast aluminium barrels will have suffered from corrosion, but sand-blasting will achieve a good finish, but they can be stove enamelled in silver which will give a better, longer lasting, appearance.

Cast iron barrels would originally have been painted gloss black. The finished barrel has been sand blasted and stove enamelled giving a strong lasting finish. With both the head and the barrel it is important to check that there are no fins missing and with the barrel, check that it has not been rebored to the maximum oversize.

The FS1-E DX front brake callipers suffer heavily from external corrosion, and the bleed nipple can become seized into the body, or worse, become sheared off. It would be advisable to take the calliper to a specialist engineer to remove the nipple.

This right-hand engine casing is definitely showing its age.

The same casing after blasting and stove enamelling.

An original head, heavily pitted, and a rusty barrel.

The same head and barrel, stove enamelled in silver and gloss black.

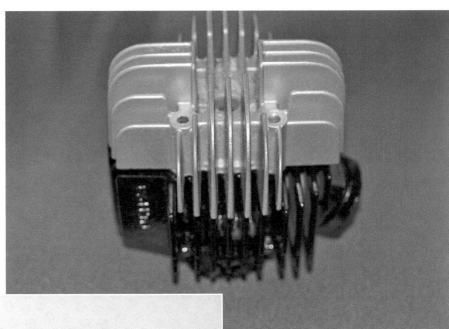

DX calipers usually turn up in a dreadful state. This example, though, isn't too bad.

The results are spectacular.

The stripped calliper and master cylinder can be sand-blasted and stove enamelled. The calliper in the accompanying picture has been refurbished and the badge has been replaced. These badges were generic to many Yamaha models of this era and some stocks are still available, but they are becoming rare.

My replica decals.

The FS1-E fork collars are likely to be rusty and are easily scratched when dismantling the forks. Some stocks are still available but are expensive.

The fork collar pictured above has been rechromed and, although the finish is good, it's not the same as the original which was slightly matt.

The finishing touch to any restoration is attention to detail and the FS1-E is no exception. I have managed to find a printing firm and have commissioned a specialist to replicate the stickers.

SEATS

Soon after embarking on the FS1-E restoration it becomes apparent which parts are rare. The cost of the parts is an instant indication. The original FS1-E seat is probably the rarest and most expensive item during the restoration, as there are very few originals left. The reason for this is the original design.

The seats comprise three main parts: the cover, the foam, and the base or pan. The pan is constructed of pressed steel and has the seat locating brackets attached to it. The foam is located on top of the pan and the cover is then stretched over the top. The cover is secured to the pan by steel spurs folded out of the pan and pushed through the cover. A decorative trim is located around the base of the cover.

The problem with the seat is simple – once the seat cover has split (which is very common) water gets in through the split and the foam acts a sponge retaining water which then causes the pan to rust. The mounting brackets fall off and, in most cases, an old seat is beyond repair.

FS1-E seats are still available but these are running low and tend to be fitted with the wider decorative band which will not suit the earlier models. (See Reference section for seat variations). These seats are also expensive.

Many people opt for the 'buddy' seat. but this was never an original fitment, looks wrong and, as stated earlier in the chapter, totally changes the lines of the FS1-E.

If the pan and foam are in acceptable condition and can be reused, then there are good quality faithful reproductions available.

If the seat is generally unserviceable then the best alternative is a quality pattern replacement. The best I have found is manufactured by P & P Seating Ltd. Its pattern seats have been designed using original seats and the results are fantastic.

While it is always preferable to use genuine parts, I consider the seat to be an exception. There is so much time and money to be wasted in refurbishing an original seat and the final result may not look as good as the replacement.

Seats suffer terribly from corrosion, once a seat cover has become split, water gets in and is absorbed into the foam. The seat base, or pan, is metal and will rust through. Additionally, the seat mounting brackets rust so badly that they become detached from the base.

A pattern seat cover.

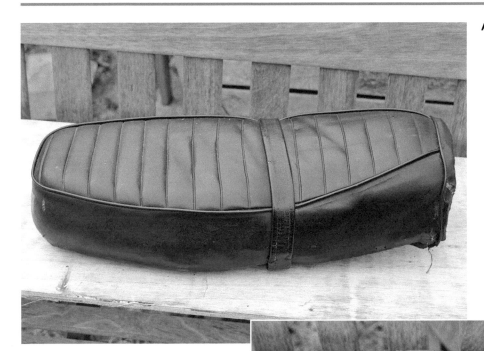

This seat pan requires major work. The pictures show the left-hand mounting bracket has gone and the rear left-hand mounting lug is also missing.

The main bracket is completely missing, and the pan is wafer thin.

The rear seat mount is also missing. It is possible to refurbish the pan with a considerable amount of welding, but as the metal is so thin this is not realistic. If the pan can be salvaged good replica seat covers are available, but in many instances a new seat is the only alternative.

The seat pictured is fitted with the early style aluminium trim but as the seats are basically the same, any style of trim can be fitted. Additionally, early seats did not have a front bracket, though these can be fitted if required.

Even the lettering is perfect.

The pan of the pattern seat is fibreglass and, therefore, will not rust, although most restored FS1-Es are unlikely to see rain!

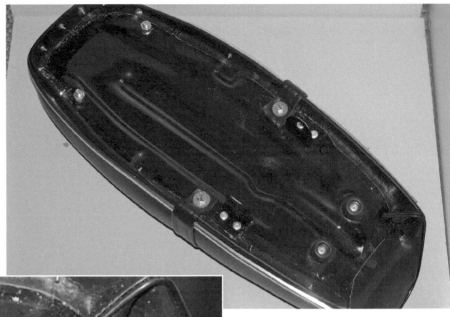

The attention to detail on this pattern seat sets it apart from most others. The rubber dampers at the front of the seat are often forgotten and, apart from the pan being fibreglass, it's difficult to tell this from an original.

The angle of the foam at the front of the seat is critical as there should be no gap between the seat and the tank. This seat mates perfectly with the tank.

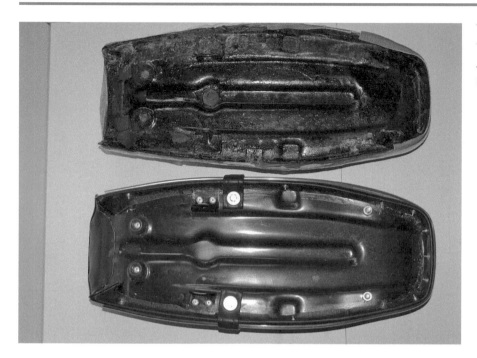

The base is moulded from an original seat and fits perfectly onto the FS1-E. It can be clearly seen that this pan is faithful to the original and that the original, above, is in poor condition, although is in no way a 'bad' one!

A cheap option is the 'buddy' style seat. These were never fitted a standard, and do change the appearance of the FS1-E.

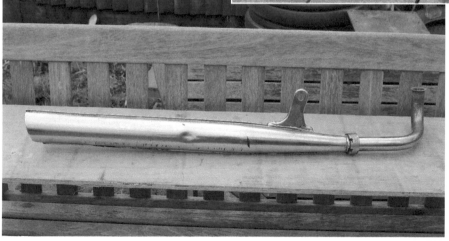

The exhaust pipe/silencer that was fitted to the early FS1-E was a one-piece assembly with a slash cut end. Apart from rust the exhaust will invariably suffer from grazing through accident damage, and will often be damaged where the kickstart pedal will have hit the side of the pipe.

The exhaust pictured will need the dents removed and the scratches polished out before rechroming.

Below: Pattern exhausts are a very good alternative. These are generally faithful to the original except for a maker's stamp on the main bracket, and the ridge is not central to the pipe.
In the FS1-E heyday, a multitude of performance accessories were available, the most popular being the expansion chamber. Opinions vary as to whether these did, in fact, improve performance, but they certainly increased the noise level! The expansion chamber pictured below is a Micron.

The numberplate fitted in the 1970s was the pressed steel type as pictured on the right; although these are no longer generally available they can still be sourced. The plate pictured on the left is the flat plastic style.

NUMBERPLATES

The rules for numberplates for the FS1-E are simple: in 1973, the appearance of numberplates was revised for the first time since 1903. From January 1st, vehicles were required to have reflective numberplates, black letters on a yellow reflective background. Prior to January 1st 1973, numberplates had a black background with white, silver or grey numbers.

The tail light/numberplate brackets often appear to be in poor condition, but these can easily be refurbished. Often the original tail light bracket has been replaced as many young owners customised their machines. Unfortunately, the result of these

This numberplate has been manufactured by Tippers Vintage Plates in original 1970s style, and has been made to fit the numberplate bracket perfectly. It is this attention to detail that will really finish off your restoration project.

The numberplate completely covers the bracket but does not oversail – this is how it should fit.

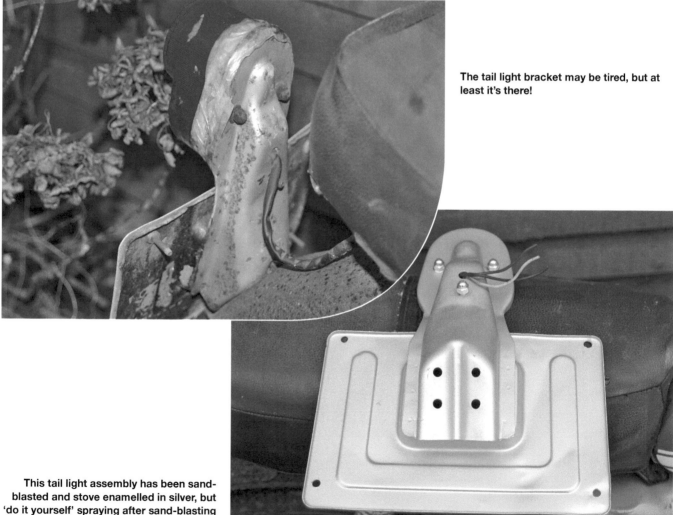

The tail light bracket may be tired, but at least it's there!

This tail light assembly has been sand-blasted and stove enamelled in silver, but 'do it yourself' spraying after sand-blasting can give excellent (and cheaper) results.

Tail light assembly. 1. Base. 2. Bulb (6v – 17/5.3W). 3. Gasket. 4. Lens. 5. Screw (x 2). 6. Numberplate bracket. 7. Dome nut (x 2). 8. Spring washer (x 2). 9. Bolt (x 4). 10. Nut (x 4). 11. Spring washer. 12. Stay. 13. Dome nut. 14. Spring washer. 15. Bolt (x 2). 16. Nut (x 2). 17. Spring washer (x 2). 18. Plain washer (x 2). (Courtesy Yamaha Motor UK)

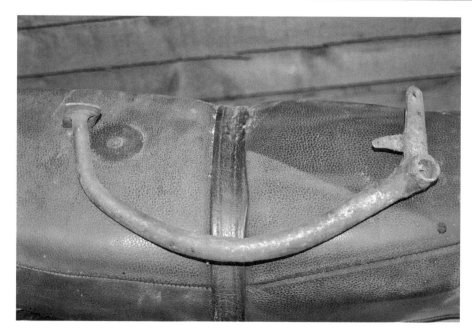

The rear brake pedal shown is in typical condition for an old FS1-E. Many other items, including the gear pedal, kickstart, rear brake arm, etc., will be in a similar state due to age and neglect. By sand-blasting and either painting, stove enamelling or zinc plating, excellent results can be achieved.

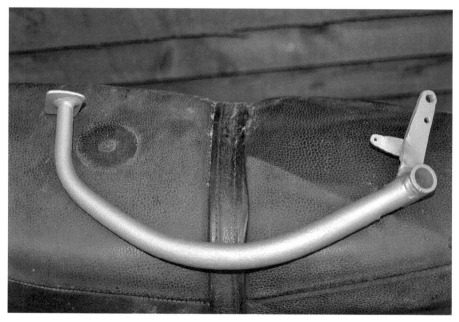

This brake pedal has been stove enamelled, although 'do it yourself' painting is a cheaper alternative.

'customisations' is that the bracket stay has become a rare and expensive item.

It is not essential to always go to motorcycle specialists to have outsourcing work carried out. For example, fireplace restoration companies will be able to carry out sand-blasting, so always think logically and shop around.

I found a local metal finishing company which was happy to carry out the restoration of all the black and silver components and engine casings, together with blasting and etch priming all the bodywork. It charged £125.00 for each FS1-E and the people there were very interested in my project.

www.velocebooks.com / www.veloce.co.uk
Details of all current books • New book news • Special offers • Gift vouchers • Forum

68

Chapter 5
Wheels

The rear wheel on this FS1-E is in reasonable condition but to really bring the bike up to concours condition it needs a lot of work. It will cost more, but having the wheels rebuilt totally changes the appearance.

With the wheel removed from the bike the quickest way to remove the spokes is by using an angle grinder.

With the hub removed, it should be degreased and, if it has been painted, remove all the old paint with paint stripper. The hubs can be refurbished by polishing using a bench grinder with polishing mops and a Dremel with a polishing attachment for the awkward areas. Polishing a hub will take time but the results are worthwhile.
Using wire wool, remove as much oxidisation as possible, which should leave a dull silver finish.
Starting with a mini drill with a polishing head, and using polishing soap, polish all the edges and intricate parts of the hub. Then use the polishing mop on the bench grinder to polish the hub. The initial results are quick but to complete each hub will take some time.

This hub is heavily corroded but can be polished.

After a lot of effort, the hub should look like this.

Wheel building

Wheel building can be undertaken by anyone but I do not do this myself, and do not recommend this is carried out by amateurs. Details of the rebuilding process are not featured in this book.

There are many wheel builders around who can often locate rims and spokes, but it pays to shop around as often these can be sourced cheaply.

The FS1-E and FS1-E DX have the same size rear wheel rims, but the front rims are different sizes. Rim sizes are detailed in the specification section of this book.

The same size differences apply to tyres.

Above: The rebuilt wheels look fantastic!

Right & below: The polished hub and new spokes are a great improvement on the tired originals.

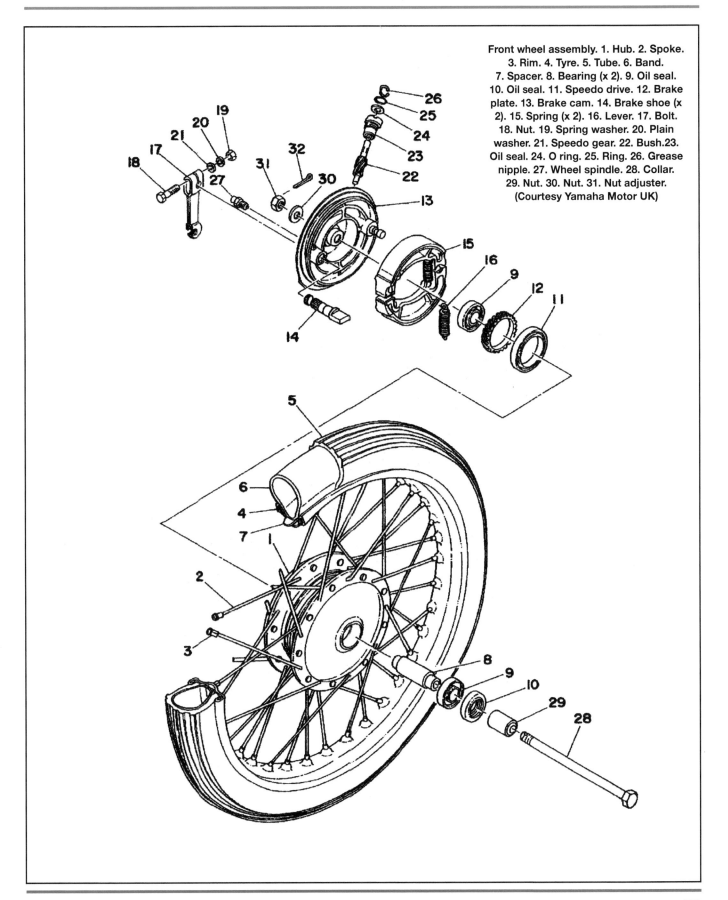

Front wheel assembly. 1. Hub. 2. Spoke. 3. Rim. 4. Tyre. 5. Tube. 6. Band. 7. Spacer. 8. Bearing (x 2). 9. Oil seal. 10. Oil seal. 11. Speedo drive. 12. Brake plate. 13. Brake cam. 14. Brake shoe (x 2). 15. Spring (x 2). 16. Lever. 17. Bolt. 18. Nut. 19. Spring washer. 20. Plain washer. 21. Speedo gear. 22. Bush.23. Oil seal. 24. O ring. 25. Ring. 26. Grease nipple. 27. Wheel spindle. 28. Collar. 29. Nut. 30. Nut. 31. Nut adjuster. (Courtesy Yamaha Motor UK)

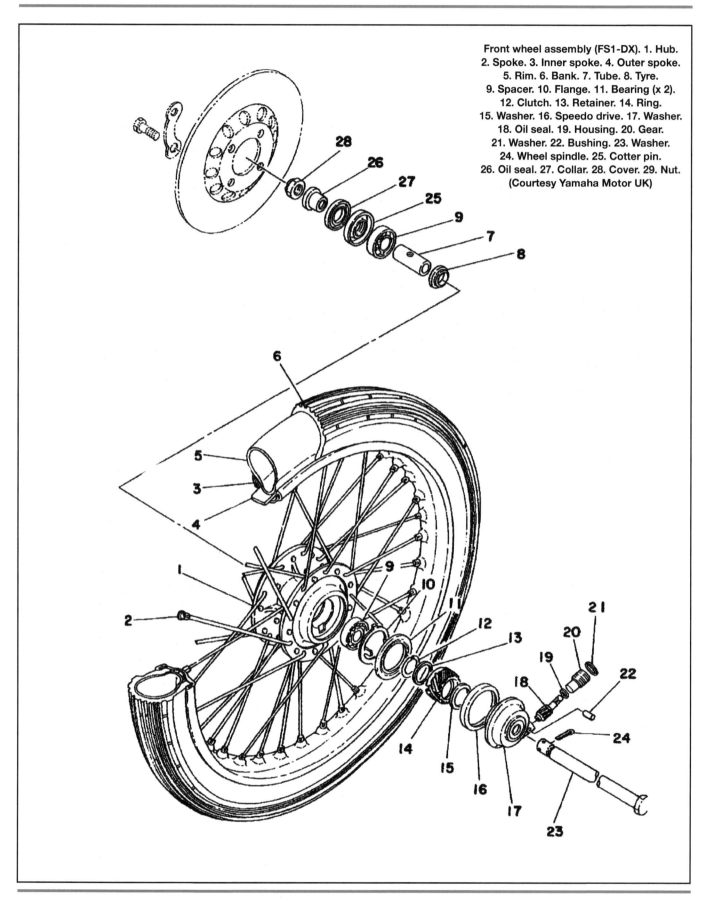

Front wheel assembly (FS1-DX). 1. Hub. 2. Spoke. 3. Inner spoke. 4. Outer spoke. 5. Rim. 6. Bank. 7. Tube. 8. Tyre. 9. Spacer. 10. Flange. 11. Bearing (x 2). 12. Clutch. 13. Retainer. 14. Ring. 15. Washer. 16. Speedo drive. 17. Washer. 18. Oil seal. 19. Housing. 20. Gear. 21. Washer. 22. Bushing. 23. Washer. 24. Wheel spindle. 25. Cotter pin. 26. Oil seal. 27. Collar. 28. Cover. 29. Nut. (Courtesy Yamaha Motor UK)

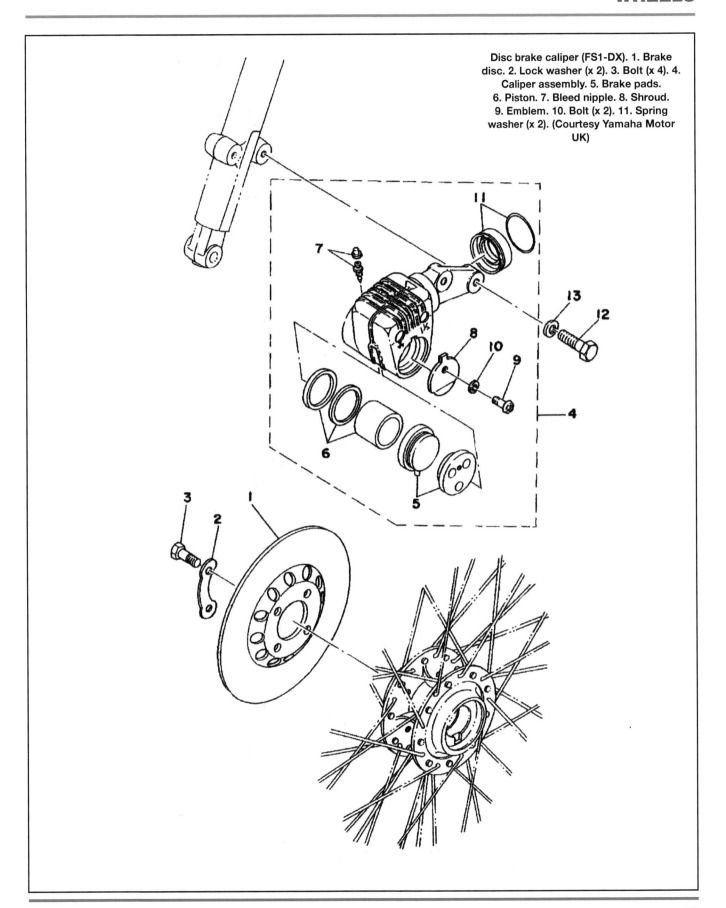

Disc brake caliper (FS1-DX). 1. Brake disc. 2. Lock washer (x 2). 3. Bolt (x 4). 4. Caliper assembly. 5. Brake pads. 6. Piston. 7. Bleed nipple. 8. Shroud. 9. Emblem. 10. Bolt (x 2). 11. Spring washer (x 2). (Courtesy Yamaha Motor UK)

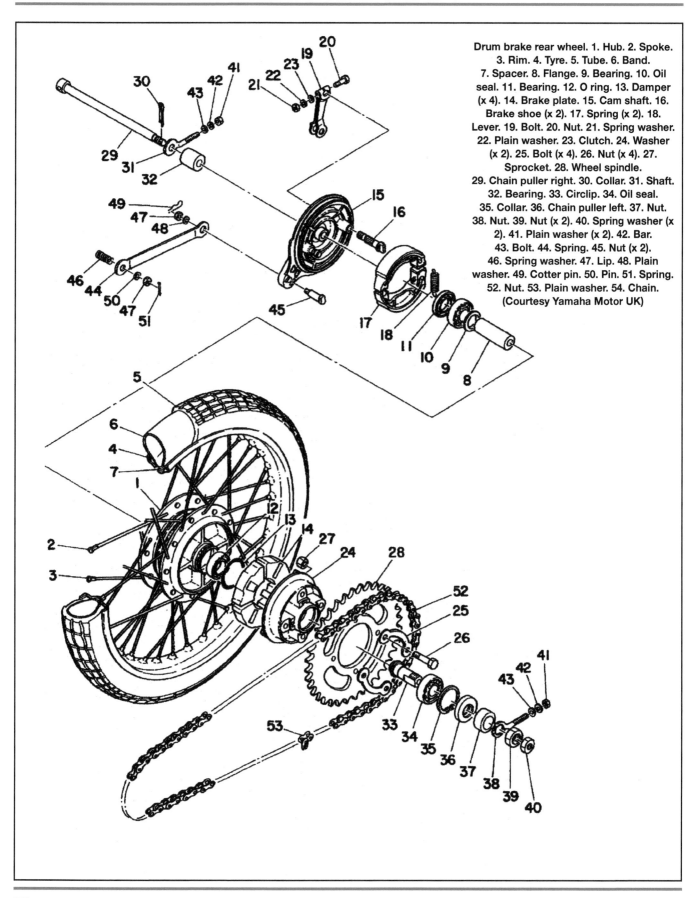

Drum brake rear wheel. 1. Hub. 2. Spoke. 3. Rim. 4. Tyre. 5. Tube. 6. Band. 7. Spacer. 8. Flange. 9. Bearing. 10. Oil seal. 11. Bearing. 12. O ring. 13. Damper (x 4). 14. Brake plate. 15. Cam shaft. 16. Brake shoe (x 2). 17. Spring (x 2). 18. Lever. 19. Bolt. 20. Nut. 21. Spring washer. 22. Plain washer. 23. Clutch. 24. Washer (x 2). 25. Bolt (x 4). 26. Nut (x 4). 27. Sprocket. 28. Wheel spindle. 29. Chain puller right. 30. Collar. 31. Shaft. 32. Bearing. 33. Circlip. 34. Oil seal. 35. Collar. 36. Chain puller left. 37. Nut. 38. Nut. 39. Nut (x 2). 40. Spring washer (x 2). 41. Plain washer (x 2). 42. Bar. 43. Bolt. 44. Spring. 45. Nut (x 2). 46. Spring washer. 47. Lip. 48. Plain washer. 49. Cotter pin. 50. Pin. 51. Spring. 52. Nut. 53. Plain washer. 54. Chain. (Courtesy Yamaha Motor UK)

Chapter 6
Electrics

The electrical systems are dealt with at length in the relevant workshop manuals and this book is not intended to replace them.

The FS1-E and FS1-E DX have very similar, simple wiring systems and all the wiring is contained within a loom. The differences between the FS1-E and the FS1-E DX relate to the handlebar switch connections and location of the ignition switch.

While there is little to go wrong with the loom, the biggest problem is that it is often 'modified' by young owners! The main modification generally comprised relocating the side ignition switch to the top location in an attempt to make the FS1-E appear to be a newer model.

The wiring loom is a fairly simple system of male and female push connectors, and if the loom is in good condition re-installing the wiring system should not be a difficult job (just follow the colour coding).

One point to watch for is adequate earthing. When rebuilding the FS1-E, ensure that there is an earth connection between items such as the headlight shroud and the shell. If you have an

The correct switchgear and the correct indicator stem length.

original shroud, you'll notice that there's no paint on the inner surface that makes contact with the shell. If yours are repainted, it may be necessary to remove some paint to achieve an earth contact.

If the loom is beyond repair, the best solution is to have the machine

rewired by a specialist. I've had my FS1-Es, when necessary, and my Z1B, rewired by Ferret from Ferret's Custom Elecktrickery. His work is first class, but one thing he does point out is that it is essential that the wiring from the magneto is installed within the frame or this will require the engine to be removed again!

Ferret has reproduced wiring looms for both the FS1-E and the FS1-E DX from original looms and has also improved upon the original design without detracting from the authenticity of the restoration.

The photographs of the Candy Gold FS1-E are included as guide for the correct lighting arrangement. It can be seen that the front indicators have shorter stems than the rear, and this also applies to the FS1-E DX.

Right: The rear indicator stems are longer than the front ones.

The left indicator in this photograph shows the difference in stem length between front and rear indicators.

Drum brake FS1-Es were fitted with switchgear on both left and right side. The FS1-E DX switchgear was all mounted on the left-hand side.

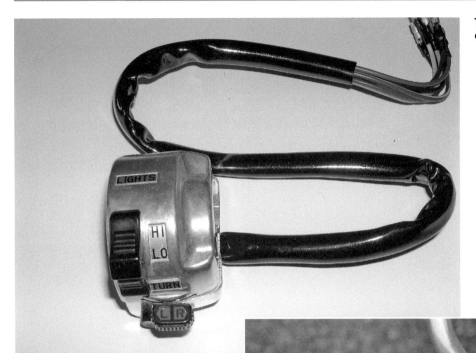

The FS1-E DX switchgear was all mounted on the left-hand side.

The top-mounted ignition switch was first introduced on the early FS1-E DX, but became the standard fitment with the introduction of the Speedblock FS1-E.

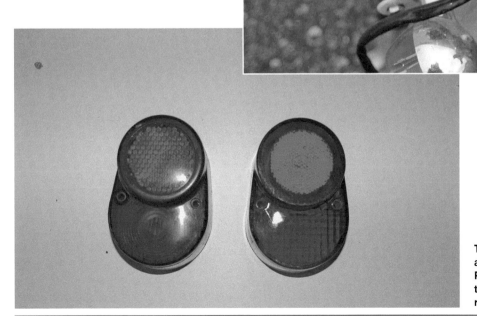

The tail light lens pictured on the left is an original, and is marked 'Stanley RR50'. Pattern lenses are available and, although they do fit, they have a totally different reflector design and carry no markings.

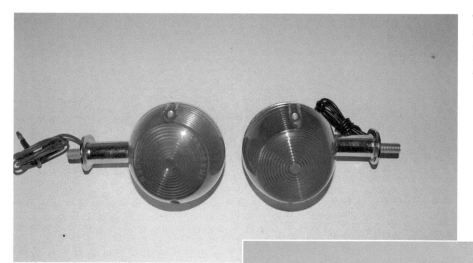

The indicator shown on the left is genuine and is marked 'Imasen'. The pattern item carries no markings on the lens and is considerably lighter in weight than the original.

The genuine Imasen lens.

The pattern lens.

Wiring loom cable colour guide		
Engine stop circuit	Black	B
Magnet (for day driving) circuit	Green	Gr
Magnet (for night driving) circuit	Yellow	Y
Battery (+) circuit	Red	R
Earth circuit	Black	B
Stop light circuit	Blue	Bl
Neutral light circuit	Sky blue	S.Bl
Light circuit	Blue	Bl
Flasher (R) circuit	Dark Green	D.Gr
Flasher (L) circuit	Dark Brown	D.Br
Common circuit	Brown	Br
Head light main circuit	Yellow	Y
Head light sub circuit	Green	Gr
Horn circuit	Pink	P
Silicon circuit (used in Selenium rectifier [-] circuit)	White	W
Flasher relay circuit	White	W
	Brown/white	Br/W
	Light/white	L.W
Ignition coil circuit (R)	Grey	G
Ignition coil circuit (L)	Orange	Or
Tail light circuit	Blue	Bl
Rear brake stop light circuit	Yellow	Y
Armature circuit	White	W
Field circuit	Green	Gr
Front brake stop light circuit	Green/yellow	Gr/Y
Light switch circuit	Red/yellow	R/Y
Head/meter light circuit	Blue (L.W.)	Bl
Ground circuit	Black	B
Rectifier circuit	White	W
Starting switch circuit	Light blue, blue/white	(CS2E only)
Starter circuit	Light green	L.Gr
AC-G (for night driving) circuit YL1	Yellow	Y
AC-G (for day driving) circuit YL1	White	W
AC-G silicon circuit (YL1)	Green	Gr
Stop lamp circuit, head light-up (YL1, YL1-E)	Blue	Bl
Daytime charging circuit (CT1, RT1)	Green	Gr
Night time charging circuit (CT1, RT1)	Green/red	Gr/R

Chapter 7
Bodywork

Depending on the project bike chosen, it will usually be necessary to refurbish the existing bodywork or locate any missing items. Breakers' yards have always been a good source for replacement items but with the continuing interest in restoration of this model, stocks are now running dry. Items on eBay have become very expensive as non-enthusiasts are exploiting genuine enthusiasts and charge inflated prices purely out of greed. Indeed, it is believed that there are individuals with stocks of new old stock spares who trickle feed parts onto the market to keep prices high!

The best way to obtain parts at a fair deal is to network with other restorers, who are genuine enthusiasts and would much rather swap parts rather than buy and sell.

The days of a good haul from a breaker's yard are over, mainly, as I stated above, due to non-enthusiasts stripping the breakers and cashing in. It is, however, worth looking as, occasionally, you'll have some luck. My wife, on one of our sourcing days, found a carburettor, four ignition switches and a petrol tap when trawling through a dirty old box of scrappy bits in the back room of a breaker's yard in Kent. She often accompanies me on these 'fishing trips' and we have picked up some important bits of kit.

The tank and side panel decals are no longer available as new parts, but there are companies that specialise in the manufacture of replicas, some are good and some are not that accurate. I had my decals produced as first editions copied from original bodywork and the results were excellent.

As I always stress, when carrying out your restoration, attention to detail is paramount to getting the perfect finish. It is, therefore, important to note that only the tank decals were lacquered over.

Matching the paint colours can be difficult too. There are companies which sell the 'right' colours, but these are not always accurate. If you can, try to build up a good relationship with your local paint sprayer as good results can be achieved at a fraction of specialist companies' prices.

Some of the most difficult items to locate, and the most expensive, are the tank badges. I have had friends in the USA trying to obtain these for me, and have visited Yamaha dealerships in every place I have been on holiday in the last four years to attempt to obtain them. Unfortunately, they are just as rare abroad as they are in the UK.

A haul like this from the breakers is a rare thing nowadays.

Popsicle Purple, Competition Yellow and Baja Brown tanks.

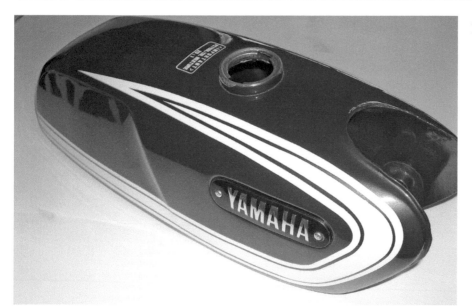

A Baja Brown tank with the very rare badge fitted.

The side panel on the right is a new old stock item, the left-hand panel has been restored, and the colour was achieved from colour matching at a local paint shop.

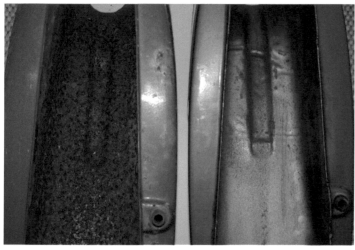

Before embarking on the restoration of the tank, it's important to check that it's not too heavily rusted internally. Even if fairly rusted inside, it can be treated by coating, but it's worth checking with a specialist as, if too heavily rusted, it may not be salvageable. If the rust is too bad, pin-holes will appear at the bottom of the tank. The two tanks pictured here are of similar age, the left-hand tank is badly rusted and is pin-holed, whereas the right-hand tank is in very good condition for its year and is ideal for restoration.

BODYWORK REPAIRS

Bodywork repairs are often best left to the specialist as, for the amateur, achieving a quality finish is not easy.

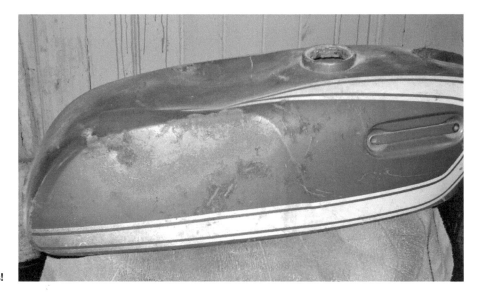

What a mess!

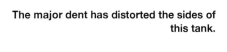

The major dent has distorted the sides of this tank.

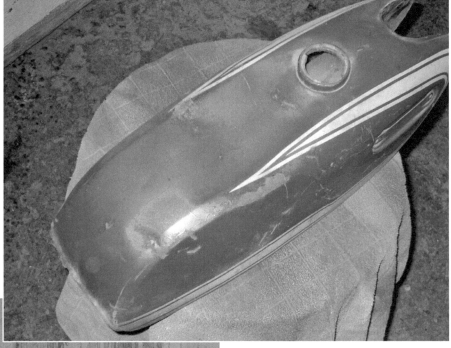

The tank is rippled all down the sides.

The Candy Gold tank pictured is in extremely poor condition, and has numerous scratches and small dents, but the major problem is the large dent on the top of the tank which has distorted the sides.

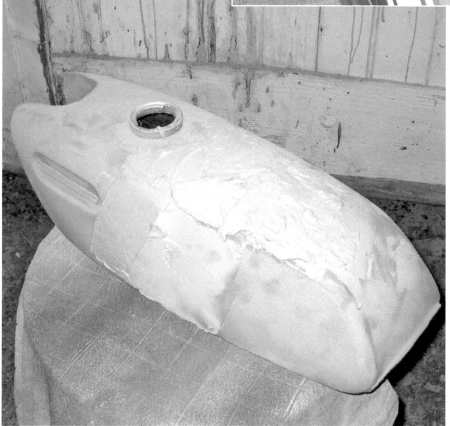

After the tank has been sand-blasted to remove the old paint, lacquer and rust, the main dent is removed as much as possible. Filler is then applied to take out any remaining imperfections.

The tank can now be rubbed down to flatten the filler and achieve the original shape. It's advisable, where possible, to have another tank on hand to refer to, and this will ensure the original contours are achieved.

The tank pictured below is in very good condition. It was bought second-hand with the intention of polishing and using as-bought. The tank is free of rust inside, and has only minor scratches that will polish out. However, in the close-up picture, it can be seen that the top of the tank has faded. The edge of the fuel mix warning sticker has come away to reveal the original colour. Despite the good overall condition, it will require repainting to achieve a really good restoration. This will still involve sand-blasting, and new paintwork and decals, as detailed in this chapter, but at least it will not require the same degree of repairs as the damaged gold tank.

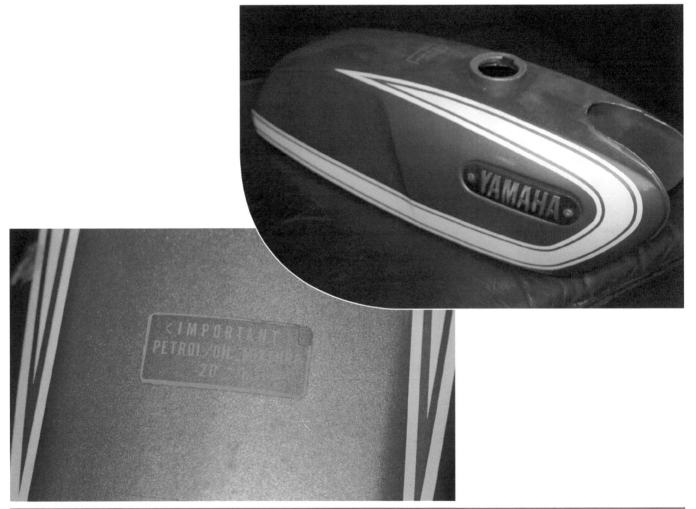

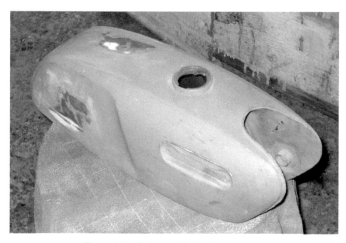

The original shape starts to reappear.

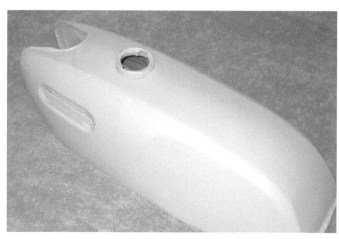

When the original shape has been achieved, the tank is then coated in a self-etch primer and rubbed down in preparation for the two-pack, high-build primer.

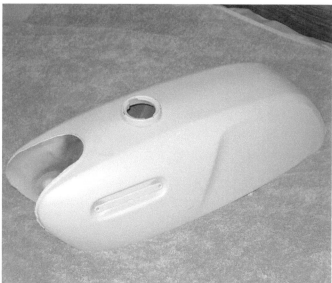

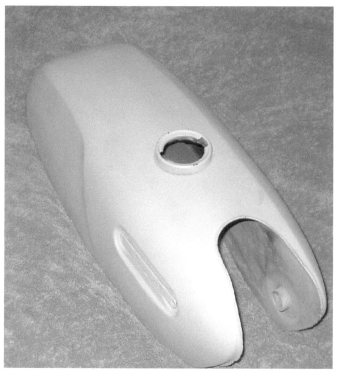

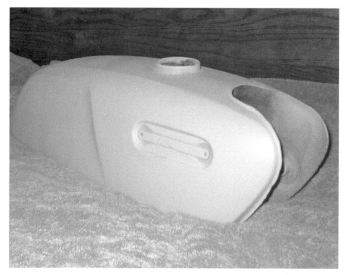

All the original lines have been restored, and from every angle the shape is now correct.

Repainting the bodywork parts does not only apply to the tank. The early FS1-E bodywork comprises tank, side panels, headlamp shell and shrouds, and shock absorber tops. The top picture shows the condition most used parts will be in prior to restoration.

After they have been sand-blasted to remove the old paint, any imperfections can be dealt with and the parts can be painted. The lower picture shows the restored parts, and the difference is amazing.

Metallic paints can vary slightly in colour between batches, and it is, therefore, always advisable to have a complete set painted together. I would recommend, therefore, waiting until the bodywork is complete before restoring it.

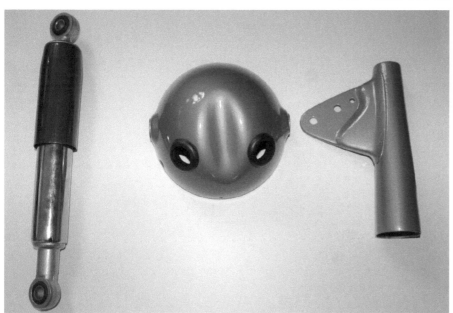

The same process applies to all other components of the bodywork. Once all these are complete the final coat can be applied.

With the tank painted the decals are the next step.

The tank should be sprayed with water. This allows the decals to be moved around to ensure they are in the correct position. Again, it's advisable to have an original tank on hand as a means of correctly placing the decals. It should be noted, however, that even the original decal locations varied from tank to tank!

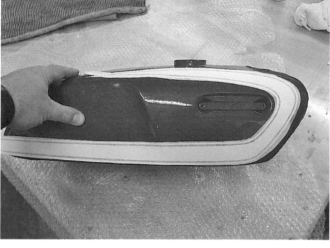

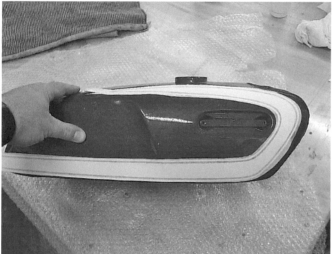

When the decal has been located and prior to removing the film, the decal must be slowly flattened using a flat plastic spatula. This process will remove air bubbles and pockets of water trapped under the decal.

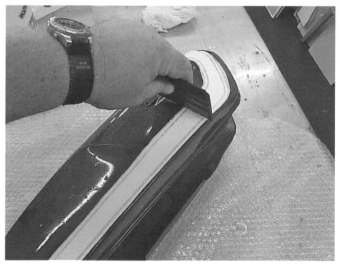

The decal can now be applied to the tank, and with the aid of the water, can be slowly moved around until the satisfactory location is achieved.

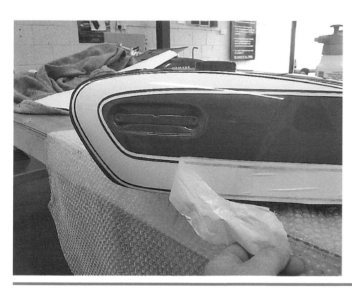

The retaining film can now be removed. It's essential not to remove this until correct positioning has been achieved, as the stripes are all separate and are correctly spaced on the film.

The decals are too long for the tank. This is designed to allow some tolerance when applying them. Fold the end of the decal around the tank and carefully trim the end using a craft knife. Be careful not to damage the paintwork.

The final process is the application of the lacquer. Remember, only the tanks were lacquered and not the side panels!

The two tanks featured in this chapter are pictured on the next page. It's hard to believe that this is the same gold tank pictured earlier in the chapter. This restoration was carried out by specialists and the results are amazing.

The completed Baja tank.

The completed Gold tank.

Year	Prefix	Colour
1973	394	Candy Gold
1974	394	Candy Gold and Popsicle Purple (R1)
1975	394	Popsicle Purple (R9) and Baja Brown
1975	596	Competition Yellow
1976	394	Baja Brown
1976	596	Competition Yellow
1977	394	Baja Brown-Speedblock
1977	596	Competition Yellow-Speedblock

www.velocebooks.com / www.veloce.co.uk
Details of all current books • New book news • Special offers • Gift vouchers • Forum

93

Chapter 8
Rebuild

This book does not deal with the details of rebuilding the Yamaha FS1-E, as this process is fully detailed in workshop manuals. The following series of photographs is intended for reference purposes when rebuilding.

With all the parts and components refurbished and located the rebuild can commence. The rebuilding process is usually far faster than imagined.

Assembling the chassis.

Installing the headlight shrouds can be difficult as the fork leg will slip through the bottom yoke and there is nothing to grip onto prior to tightening the clamp bolt. The wheel spindle has the same thread as the fork bolt and can be threaded into the fork tube and pulled up whilst the lower clamp bolt is tightened.

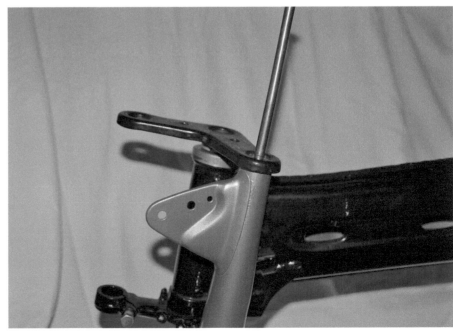

Right- and left-hand views of a completed machine.

Pay particular attention to using the correct nuts and bolts. The tail light bracket stay bolts are often located using Phillips head screws, the correct bolts are used here.

The seat trim varies between models. This early example has the thinner, rounded base trim; later models were fitted with the wider, flat trim. After August 1977, seat trim was body-coloured.

New old stock exhausts are very rare. Originals can be rechromed but, in most instances, a pattern exhaust is the only option. The pattern exhausts are fairly cheap and easy to obtain. They differ from genuine exhausts in that they are stamped on the main bracket, and the top rib is located slightly to the right rather than on the top of the silencer. This example has a new old stock exhaust.

The air box has two cable retaining lugs which are often missing. Although this does not affect the completed machine, it's preferable to locate an air box with both lugs.

This example has a modern plug cap. The original fitment was a metal type. These were one of the few problems owners experienced, as they were unreliable in wet weather. It is advisable to use a modern plug cap if the machine is to be ridden in rain, though most restored FS1-Es are rarely ridden, especially in the wet!

The carburettor is the correct type for this early FS1-E, as it is fitted with the cable choke. All models with side ignition were fitted with this type; all DXs and top ignition models had carburettor-mounted chokes.

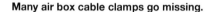

Many air box cable clamps go missing.

Rear wheel/brake detail.

The correct kickstart lever will clear the exhaust.

The correct finish to the pedal guard and chain guard.

The early model brake plate was located on the right-hand side.

Attention to detail is essential.

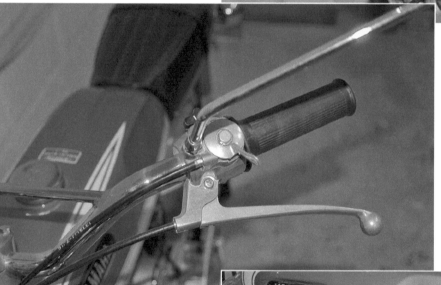

The left-hand switch gear, with correct choke lever and bolt, and the correct grips.

Ignition side detail.

Cables must be routed correctly.

Many FS1-Es ended up with the wrong nuts and bolts in this area. The photograph details the correct arrangement.

Right-hand brake, as fitted to the early FS1-E.

Chapter 9
Reference

The purpose of this chapter is to provide a reference for the would-be restorer to establish the model they wish to restore, and a guide to the correct specification of their machine.

It is important to research the machine you intend to restore and familiarize yourself with the specification of that chosen model. If not researched adequately, many parts and components will be purchased incorrectly and money will be wasted.

There are many members on the FS1-E website (www.fs1e.co.uk) who will own the model you intend to restore and will usually be willing to offer advice and assistance with your restoration.

The accompanying pictures show the earliest FS1-E, which originally had 'SS' on the side panels. This version was introduced in August 1972, and the earliest examples in the UK were L registration. Until August 1973, they were only available in Candy Gold. Between August 1972 and 1973, the side panel stickers were changed to read FS1-E.

From August 1974, Yamaha introduced Popsicle Purple and, apart from some Candy Gold models unsold,

most FS1-Es were sold in the new colour. There are two Popsicle Purples and the Yamaha reference for these is R1 and R9.

In August 1975, Yamaha changed the FS1-E colour to Baja Brown, and the Popsicle Purple models were no longer produced. At the same time, the first FS1-E DX was introduced. The main differences between the FS1-E and the DX model was the introduction of the top-mounted ignition, totally different front forks, hydraulic disc brake, and unbraced handlebars. This version was called the FS1-ED or FS1-D, but was generally known as the FS1-E DX.

Between August 1975 and August 1976 the FS1-E had a major facelift. Both the FS1-E and the DX were fitted with the top-mounted ignition, the headlamp shell and shrouds were painted black instead of tank colour, the shock absorbers were changed to the exposed spring type, and the tank was revised. The fuel tank became wider and was no longer fitted with the screw on badges, and the decals were revised with the speedblock design with '50' on the side panels.

The FS1-E was available in Baja Brown and the DX in Competition Yellow.

The sales brochure reproduced here shows the mid-1976, facelift DX model, though the model shown was not faithful to the UK specification. The discrepancies are: the tail light assembly is incorrect, as this was identical to the earlier models; the exhaust pipe is a two-piece system and does not have the correct slash cut end; the handlebars are a higher rise than the UK specification; and the DX was not available in the UK in blue.

The second major facelift occurred in 1977, with the introduction of the Auto-lube models. A point that the restorer should be aware of is that, although the differences appear cosmetic, many components are not interchangeable. As described earlier in this book, the fork tubes are not the same as early models and will not fit, and the front and rear mudguards are different. The early front mudguards are designed to suit the right-hand brake plate and, therefore, have the cable damper on the opposite side to the later models. Rear mudguards do not have

the cable tunnel as the tail light assembly is different.

The fuel tap is located further forward to allow for the longer plastic side panels.

The swinging arm has rear footrest brackets welded to the arm rather than the earlier threaded type.

The speedometer is plastic instead of the chrome finish on the early models.

The chrome seat trim is body coloured.

Indicators are a different shape.

The later DX model has a revised caliper and master cylinder.

The rear shock absorbers have a small chrome shroud at the top, and the lower mounting lugs have a smaller diameter hole.

The first FS1-E or SS.

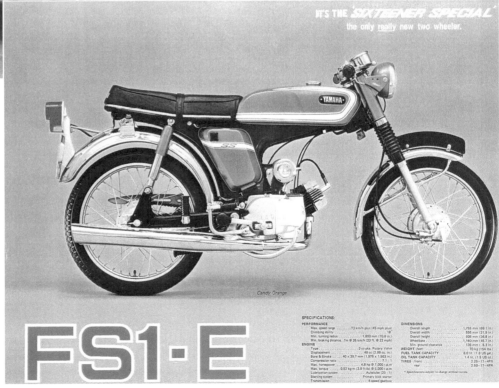

Page from the first brochure.

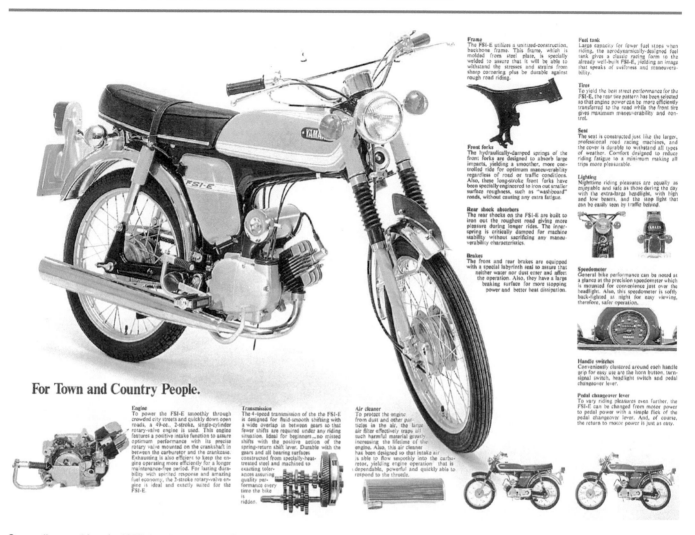

For Town and Country People.

Engine
To power the FS1-E smoothly through crowded city streets and quickly down open roads, a 49-cc., 2-stroke, single-cylinder rotary-valve engine is used. This engine features a positive intake function to assure optimum performance with its precise rotary valve mounted on the crankshaft in between the carburetor and the crankcase. Exhausting is also efficient to keep the engine operating more efficiently for a longer maintenance-free period. For lasting durability with spirited response and amazing fuel economy, the 2-stroke rotary-valve engine is ideal and exactly suited for the FS1-E.

Transmission
The 4-speed transmission of the the FS1-E is designed for fluid-smooth shifting with a wide overlap in between gears so that fewer shifts are required under any riding situation. Ideal for beginners...no missed shifts with the positive action of the spring-return shift lever. Durable with the gears and all bearing surfaces constructed from specially-heat-treated steel and machined to exacting tolerances assuring quality performance every time the bike is ridden.

Air cleaner
To protect the engine from dust and other particles in the air, the large air filter effectively traps all such harmful material greatly increasing the lifetime of the engine. Also, this air cleaner has been designed so that intake air is able to flow smoothly into the carburetor, yielding engine operation that is dependable, powerful and quickly able to respond to the throttle.

Frame
The FS1-E utilizes a unitized-construction, backbone frame. This frame, which is molded from steel plate, is specially welded to assure that it will be able to withstand the stresses and strains from sharp cornering plus be durable against rough road riding.

Front forks
The hydraulically-damped springs of the front forks are designed to absorb large impacts, yielding a smoother, more controlled ride for optimum maneuverability regardless of road or traffic conditions. Also, these long-stroke front forks have been specially-engineered to iron out smaller surface roughness, such as "washboard" roads, without causing any extra fatigue.

Rear shock absorbers
The rear shocks on the FS1-E are built to iron out the roughest road giving more pleasure during longer rides. The inner-spring is critically damped for machine stability without sacrificing any maneuverability characteristics.

Brakes
The front and rear brakes are equipped with a special labyrinth seal to assure that neither water nor dust enter and affect the operation. Also, they have a large braking surface for more stopping power and better heat dissipation.

Fuel tank
Large capacity for fewer fuel stops when riding, the aerodynamically-designed fuel tank gives a classic racing form to the already well-built FS1-E, yielding an image that speaks of swiftness and maneuverability.

Tires
To yield the best street performance for the FS1-E, the rear tire pattern has been selected so that engine power can be more efficiently transferred to the road while the front tire gives maximum maneuverability and control.

Seat
The seat is constructed just like the larger, professional road racing machines, and the cover is durable to withstand all types of weather. Comfort designed to reduce riding fatigue to a minimum making all trips more pleasurable.

Lighting
Nighttime riding pleasures are equally as enjoyable and safe as those during the day with the extra-large headlight, with high and low beams, and the stop light that can be easily seen by traffic behind.

Speedometer
General bike performance can be noted at a glance at the precision speedometer which is mounted for convenience just over the headlight. Also, this speedometer is softly back-lighted at night for easy viewing, therefore, safer operation.

Handle switches
Conveniently clustered around each handle grip for easy use are the horn button, turn-signal switch, headlight switch and pedal changeover lever.

Pedal changeover lever
To vary riding pleasures even further, the FS1-E can be changed from motor power to pedal power with a simple flick of the pedal changeover lever. And, of course, the return to motor power is just as easy.

Generally speaking, in 1975 the drum brake FS1-E was sold in Baja Brown, as shown in the small picture in the bottom right-hand corner of the brochure. Very small numbers of the Yellow and Blue models were sold in the UK.

This is the earliest disc brake version, sold generally in the UK in Competition Yellow, and in small numbers in Blue. Although this was known as the FS1-E DX, it was officially the FS1-ED, and did not become the FS1-E DX until it was sold in the Speedblock livery.

FS1-E DX with Speedblock livery on the fuel tank.

FS1-EDX 'Kenny Roberts'.

YAMAHA FS1DX

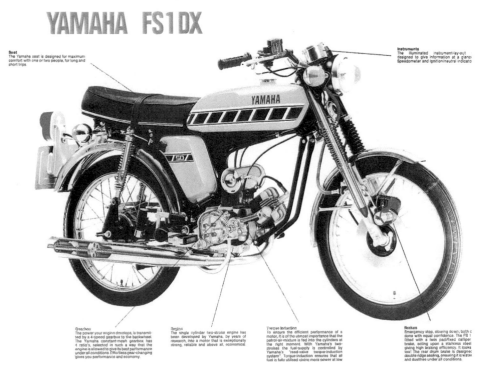

Seat
The Yamaha seat is designed for maximum comfort with one or two people, for long and short trips.

Instruments
The illuminated instrument-lay-out designed to give information at a glance. Speedometer and ignition/neutral indicator.

Gearbox
The power your engine develops, is transmitted by a 4-speed gearbox to the backwheel. The Yamaha constant-mesh gearbox has 4 ratio's, selected in such a way that the engine is allowed to give its best performance under all conditions. Effortless gear-changing gives you performance and economy.

Engine
The single cylinder two-stroke engine has been developed by Yamaha, by years of research, into a motor that is exceptionally strong, reliable and above all, economical.

Torque Induction
To ensure the efficient performance of a motor, it is of the utmost importance that the petrol-air-mixture is fed into the cylinders at the right moment. With Yamaha's two-strokes the fuel-supply is controlled by Yamaha's 'reed-valve torque-induction system'. Torque-induction ensures that all fuel is fully utilised giving more power at low

Brakes
Emergency stop, slowing down, both can done with equal confidence. The FS1 fitted with a twin pad/fixed caliper brake, acting upon a stainless steel giving high braking efficiency. It looks too! The rear drum brake is designed double ridge sealing, ensuring it is water and dustfree under all conditions.

Below: This is the end of the line for the pedal models, although the pedals were replaced with footrest style pedals. Other minor changes included plastic speedo, restyled indicators, plastic side panels and revised tail light.
Other less noticeable changes were revised rear brake pedal, and the front brake hub was moved from the right to the left. The livery also changed, and was also available in Red. The major change was the introduction of the Autolube system.

The new generation restricted FS1. Changes included restyled caliper and master cylinder and livery, but generally the same appearance as the last of the pedal models.

The drum brake version of the first restricted model.

The FS1 DX and FS1 mark the first major styling change. Restyled tank, side panel and seat. It is difficult to recognise the early FS1-E by now.

The FS1-SE. A rare chopper version which was sold in small numbers and has become quite desirable.

RESTORED EXAMPLES

The following photographs are a collection of good examples of FS1-Es that exist today and are included for reference.

The FS1-E above is a 1973-74 vintage in the early 'SS' form. Generally, these were not fitted with indicators as standard, as they were an optional extra. This example is in superb condition. The only, and in my opinion sensible deviation from standard, is the plastic sparkplug cap.

This example is finished in the popular Popsicle Purple and is from the 1974 to 1975 era. It is in excellent condition and, apart from the plastic sparkplug cap is faithful to the original specification.

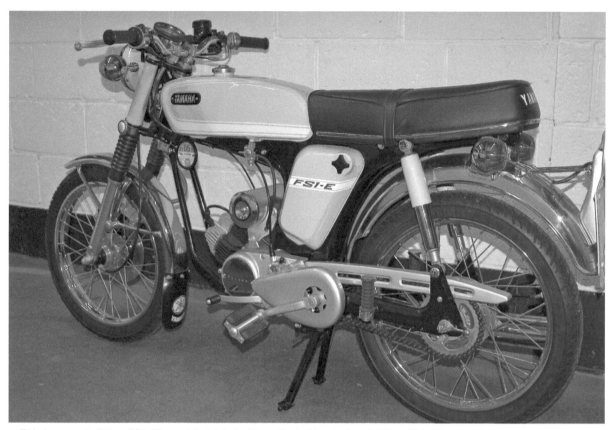

This is an early **DX** or **FS1-ED** model which, incidentally, is identical to the first FS1-E I owned in 1977. This example is perfect in every detail.

These two photographs are of the FS1-E DX with the 'Speedblock' or 'Kenny Roberts' tank livery, and would have been sold from August 1976 onward.

This example is finished in the early Baja Brown livery. This model would have originally been fitted with a standard seat. The restoration of this machine has been expertly carried out and it is a beautiful example, except that the pedals have been replaced with a footrest bar.

This 1975 Popsicle Purple model is excellent, except for the non-standard seat and lack of pedal gear.

This 1977 Baja Brown drum brake model is almost perfect. Even the sparkplug cap is original.

One minor issue concerns the pattern front mudguard, which is slightly too large.

FS1-E MODEL REFERENCE – 1972 TO 1992

Model	Prefix	Year	Colour	Tank Styling	Pedals	Restricted
FS1-E	394	1972-1974	Candy Gold	Pin Stripe Decals. Screw-on badges	Yes	No
FS1-E	394	1974-1976	Popsicle Purple	Pin Stripe Decals. Screw-on badges	Yes	No
FS1-E	394	1975-1976	Baja Brown	Pin Stripe Decals. Screw-on badges	Yes	No
FS1-ED	596	1975-1976	Competion Yellow	Pin Stripe Decals. Screw-on badges	Yes	No
FS1-E	394	1976-1977	Baja Brown	Speedblock Decals	Yes	No
FS1-E DX	596	1976-1977	Competion Yellow	Speedblock Decals.	Yes	No
FS1E-A	394	1977	Space Blue	Revised Speedblock Decals	Yes	No
FS1E-DXA	394	1977	Chappy Red	Revised Speedblock Decals	Yes	No
FS1-M	2GO	1977-1979	French Blue Metallic	Revised Speedblock Decals	No	Yes
FS1-M DX	2GO	1977-1983	Wineberry Red	Revised Speedblock Decals	No	Yes
FS1	3F6	1987-1992	Caribbean Blue	White Blocks	No	Yes
FS1DX	3F6	1978-1983	Maxim Red	Black Blocks	No	Yes
FS1-SE	5A1	1981 -1983	Yamaha Black	-	No	Yes

FS1-E MODEL HISTORY

1972	The SS 'Sixteener Special' launched in the UK in August. Finished in Candy Gold.
1973	January, the SS side panel decal was changed to FS1-E. August, the colour finish was changed to Popsicle Purple.
1975	Popsicle Purple models still available. August, Baja Brown finish introduced. FS1-ED launched. The livery was identical to current model, but finished in Competition Yellow. The original forks were replaced with uprated stronger type, hydraulic disc brake and the ignition switch was relocated from the side panel to a switch adjacent to the speedometer. The braced handlebars were replaced with lower bars and the handlebar switches were replaced with a single switch located on the left, which no longer incorporated the choke lever as the revised carburettor had a pull up choke mechanism.
1976	FS1-E revised cosmetically. The original tank was replaced with wider version without the screw on badges and the livery changed to black and white Speed Block graphics on Baja Brown paintwork. The headlamp shell and shrouds now black and the shock absorbers replaced with open spring type. Also wider seat trim. The ignition switch from the FS1-ED adopted for all models. FS1-ED replaced with the FS1-E DX. Generally as the FS1-ED, finished in Competition Yellow but sporting the revised cosmetics as the 1976 FS1-E.
1977	1976 models available unchanged until August 1977. August, FS1-E replaced with the first restricted FS1 Autolube model. Pedal mechanism still fitted but the original bicycle pedals replaced with smaller footrest style type. Various other changes included; plastic side speedometer and side panels, flatter chrome indicators, body coloured seat trim, revised tail light and small chrome shrouds at the top of the rear shock absorbers. The front brake plate switched from right side to left. Available in Space Blue. FS1 Disc brake version, as above, but available in Chappy Red. Also front brake calliper no longer fitted with separate badge and master cylinder replaced with square version.
1978	FS1-A, drum brake, and FS1-DXA models introduced. Identical to the previous models except for the colour scheme and livery. The FS1-A available in Caribbean Blue and the FS1-DXA available in Wineberry Red.
1981	FS1-SE introduced the first Chopper style moped, known as the 'Custom'. Available in Maxim Red and Yamaha Black.
1983	FS1-A and FS1-DXA finally discontinued in the 1978 form.
1987-1993	The FS1 reintroduced in its final form. This model looked radically different from all the previous models. The tank was totally redesigned in a much squarer shape and the seat incorporated a coloured tail section. The final version included yellow fork gaiters and shock absorbers and was available in Red for the disc brake version and Blue for the drum brake.

www.velocebooks.com / www.veloce.co.uk
Details of all current books • New book news • Special offers • Gift vouchers • Forum

115

Chapter 10
Clubs, suppliers & specialists

CLUBS

FS1-E Owners Club
Yew Tree Cottage
Longhill Lane
Audlem
Cheshire
CW3 0HU
Tel: 01270 842 037
Website: www.fs1eoc.co.uk
Email: info@fs1eoc.co.uk

Sports Moped Owners Club
Secretary: Chris Alty
14a Kestrel Park
Ashurst
Skelmersdale
Lancashire
WN8 6TB

Yamaha Classic Club
Website: yamahaclub.com

Yamaha Owners Club
yamahaownersclub.org.uk

Yamaha Riders Club
Secretary: Christine Kemp
9 Filland Court
Sandy

Bedfordshire
SG19 1HW

Vintage Japanese Motorcycle Club
(VJMC)
PO Box 14
Corwen
LL21 9WF
Website: www.vjmc.com

FS1-E Website
Webmaster: Andy Naughton-Doe
www.fs1e.co.uk

FS1-E Register
Nick Warner
E-mail: nickwar@btinternet.com

SUPPLIERS AND SPECIALISTS
Seats

P and P Seating Ltd.
429 The Meadway
Birmingham
B33 0DZ
United Kingdom
Tel: 0121 784 4001
Email: info@ppseat.co.uk
Website: facebook.com/PPSeat/

Spare parts

Motomax
65 High Street
Caterham
Surrey
CR3 5UF
Tel: 01883 330049
Fax: 01883 330655

Fizzy Galore
76 Halifax Old Road
Birkby
Huddersfield
West Yorkshire
HD1 6HG
Tel: 01484 548593
Fax: 01484 420280
E-mail: russ.marsden@ntlworld.com
Website: www.fs1egalore.co.uk

Decals

Sussex Sign Company
2-4 Foredown Drive
Portslade
East Sussex
BN41 2BB
Tel: 01273 258506
Email: info@sussexsigns.com
Website: sussexsigns.com

Bodywork

Paul's Bodyshop
Unit 4
No.1 Cuthbert Road
Westgate on Sea
Kent
CT8 8NR
Tel: 01843 833111
Website: www.paulsbodyshop.co.uk

Welding/frame repairs

J Colburn Metal Fabrications
Aldrington Basin South
Portslade
Sussex
BN41 1WF
Tel: 01273 413190
Website: jcolburns.co.uk
Email: jcolburn@garthco.uk

Classic numberplates

Tippers Vintage Plates
Unit 2, Bucklers Lane
St Austell
Cornwall
PL25 3JN
Tel: 01726 879799
Fax: 01726 871413
Website: tippersvintageplates.co.uk
Email: tippersplates@gmail.com

Wiring

Ferret's Custom Elecktrickery
Tel: 07765 832420
Website: motorcyclewiring.co.uk

Chromium plating

Collins Chemical Blacking
5 & 6b Aultone Yard
Aultone Way
Carshalton
Surrey SM5 2LH
Tel/Fax: 020 8647 3123
Website: collinschemicalblacking.co.uk

Powder coating/sandblasting

Microblast Powder Coating
Microblast Services Ltd
Old Yard Workshop
Vansittart Estate
Arthur Road
Windsor
Berkshire
SL4 1SE
Tel: 01753 620145
Website: microblastservices.co.uk
Email: enquiries@microblastservices.co.uk

www.velocebooks.com / www.veloce.co.uk
Details of all current books • New book news • Special offers • Gift vouchers • Forum

117

Chapter 11
Conclusion

All of the FS1-E models covered in this book were built to be used, and so, once restored, you should not be afraid to use your Fizzy. Part of the pleasure of ownership for a good many enthusiasts is 'tinkering' with their toy in order to keep it in fine condition and, perhaps, improving detail when the opportunity arises.

Although Chapter 1 specifically deals with choosing the FS1-E you wish to restore, you may not have too much choice as these machines are much sought after, and your options may be limited to the few machines or major components available at any one time.

The primary consideration has to be that you have the correct frame for your desired restoration, i.e., if you want a pedal, unrestricted drum brake version, make sure you have a 394 prefix frame and engine. Once this has been achieved you know you have the correct platform for your restoration and the remaining parts can be sourced from elsewhere.

I hope this book is useful, and that it gives you a good insight into the highs and lows of a restoration without wasting money on incorrect parts.

So, have fun, on and off the road. The biggest problem with riding your completed FS1-E will be that you are constantly stopped by ex-owners who will want to reminisce about their Fizzy!

www.velocebooks.com / www.veloce.co.uk
Details of all current books • New book news • Special offers • Gift vouchers • Forum

118

Appendix
Specifications

High-performance rotary valve engine	Yamaha's 2–stroke rotary valve engine provides stable performance at low speed and smooth running at high speed as well as maximum acceleration at all speeds.
Easy starting	The engine can also be started by simply pulling in the clutch lever and kicking the starter without shifting the transmission gear back to neutral.
Sturdy 7–bone style frame	The design of the frame provides greater strength for both off and on the road riding.
Larger lights	Large tail lights along with the easy–check speedometer ensure additional safety for riders in heavy traffic.
Easy start feature	The starting feature within the carburettor assures easy starting in all types of weather.
Powerful brakes	Patented waterproof and dustproof brake drums provide safe, fade free braking on wet or dusty roads, and hydraulic disc brake on the FS1-ED and FS1-DX models.

Specifications courtesy of Yahama Motor UK.

SPECIFICATIONS

Full specifications are given in the following tables.

FS1-E specifications	
Dimensions: Overall length Overall width Overall height Wheelbase Minimum ground clearance	 69.1in (1755 mm) 21.9in (555 mm) 36.8in (935 mm) 45.7in (1160 mm) 5.3in (135 mm)
Weight (net)	155lb (70kg)
Performance: Maximum speed Fuel consumption (on level paved roads) Climbing ability Minimum turning radius Braking distance	 45mph (73km/h) 188 mile/US gal. 19mph (80km at 30km/h) 18in (457mm) 70.9in (1800 mm) 23ft/22mph (7m/35km/h)
Engine: Engine type/model Lubricating system/mixing ratio Cylinder arrangement Displacement Bore and stroke Compression ratio Maximum output Maximum torque Starting method Ignition method Carburetor Air cleaner	 2-stroke, gasoline, air cooled Mixed fuel of gasoline and oil 20:1 Single, forward inclined $2.99in^3$ (49cc) 1.575in x 1.563in (40mm x 39.7mm) 7.1:1 4.8bhp/7000rpm (4.8ps/7000rpm) 3.8ft/lb/6000rpm (0.52kg-m/6000rpm) Kickstarter Flywheel magneto VM-16SC Dry, paper filter
Power transmission: Clutch Primary reduction method Primary reduction ratio Transmission	 Wet, multi-disc Gear 3.895 (74/19) 4-speed, constant mesh
Gear ratios: 1st 2nd 3rd 4th Secondary reduction method Secondary reduction ratio	 3.077 1.899 1.304 1.038 Chain 2.785 (39/14)
Chassis: Frame Models Suspension (front) Suspension (rear)	 Pressed steel backbone 394/596 Telescopic forks incorporating coil springs and shock absorbers Swing arm and coil spring/shock absorber units
Steering: Caster Trail	 63.5° 3.0in (75.6mm)

Brakes: Type Operation method (front) Operation method (rear) 394 series models 596 series models	Internal expansion Right hand-operation Right foot-operation Drum type front brake, drum rear Disk type front brake, drum rear
Tyres: Front Rear	2.25 (2.50 DX) – 17 – 4PR 2.50 – 17 – 4PR
Fuel tank capacity	1.33 Imperial gallons (6.05 litres/1.6 US gallons)
Oil tank capacity	0.307 Imperial gallon (1.4 litres/1.5 US quarts)
Generator: Model Manufacturer	FAZ-1QL or F11-L40 Mitsubishi Electric or Hitachi
Sparkplug	B-7HS
Battery: Model Capacity	BST2-6 6 volt, 4 amp hour
Lights: Headlight Tail/stoplight Neutral light Meter light	6 volt 18w/18w 6 volt 5w/21w 6 volt 3w 6 volt 1.5w

Engine stop circuit	Black	B
Magnet (for day driving) circuit	Green	Gr
Magnet (for night driving) circuit	Yellow	Y
Battery (+) circuit	Red	R
Earth circuit	Black	B
Stop light circuit	Blue	Bl
Neutral light circuit	Sky blue	S.Bl
Light circuit	Blue	Bl
Flasher (R) circuit	Dark Green	D.Gr
Flasher (L) circuit	Dark Brown	D.Br
Common circuit	Brown	Br
Head light main circuit	Yellow	Y
Head light sub circuit	Green	Gr
Horn circuit	Pink	P
Silicon circuit (used in	White	W
Selenium rectifier (-) circuit (used in		
Flasher relay circuit	White Brown/white Light/white	W Br/W L.W
Ignition coil circuit (R)	Grey	G
Ignition coil circuit (L)	Orange	Or

Tail light circuit	Blue	Bl
Rear brake stop light circuit	Yellow	Y
Armature circuit	White	W
Field circuit	Green	Gr
Front brake stop light circuit	Green/yellow	Gr/Y
Light switch circuit	Red/yellow	R/Y
Head/meter light circuit	Blue (L.W.)	Bl
Ground circuit	Black	B
Rectifier circuit	White	W
Starting switch circuit	Light blue, blue/white	(CS2E only)
Starter circuit	Light green	L.Gr
AC-G (for night driving) circuit YL1	Yellow	Y
AC-G (for day driving) circuit YL1	White	W
AC-G silicon circuit (YL1)	Green	Gr
Stop lamp circuit, head light-up (YL1, YL1-E)	Blue	Bl
Daytime charging circuit (CT1, RT1)	Green	Gr
Night-time charging circuit (CT1, RT1)	Green/red	Gr/R

www.velocebooks.com / www.veloce.co.uk
Details of all current books • New book news • Special offers • Gift vouchers • Forum

122

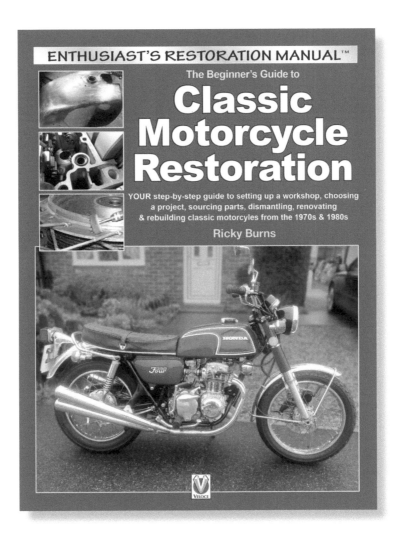

Seasoned motorcycle restorer Ricky Burns goes through each of the stages of a real-life restoration. Aimed at the total beginner but suitable for enthusiasts of all abilities, the reader is taken through each step in detail, and taught the techniques, tricks and tips used by experts. From choosing a project, setting up a workshop, and preparing a bike, to sourcing parts, dismantling, restoring and renovating, this book is the perfect guide for the classic motorcycle restorer.

ISBN: 978-1-845846-44-2
Paperback • 27x20.7cm • 144 pages • 594 pictures

ALSO FROM VELOCE PUBLISHING –

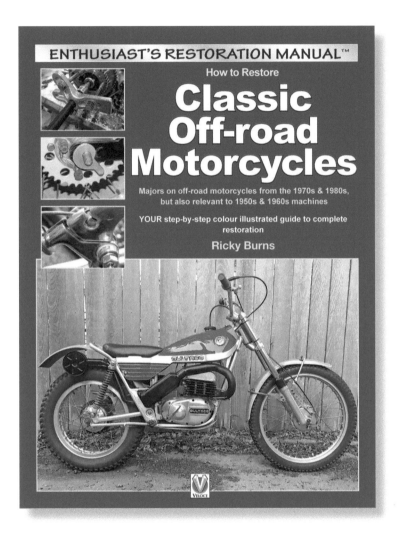

How to Restore Classic Off-road Motorcycles provides the classic off-road enthusiast with a step-by-step guide through a full restoration. Whether a post-1950 machine, or a more modern '80s twin shock, everything is covered in detail, from initial dismantling and parts sourcing to being ready to compete, including set-up and maintenance.

ISBN: 978-1-845849-50-4
Paperback • 27x20.7cm • 160 pages • 488 colour pictures

For more information and price details, visit our website at www.veloce.co.uk • email: info@veloce.co.uk
• Tel: +44(0)1305 260068

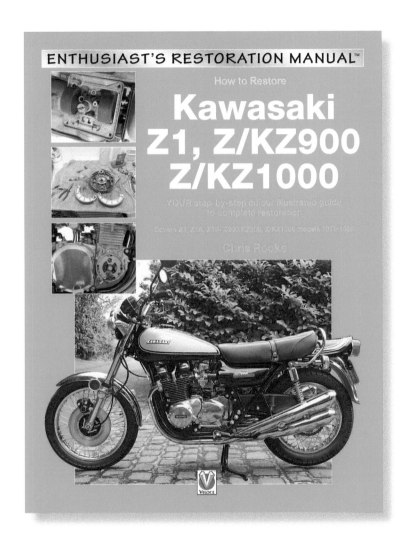

Written in a friendly and engaging manner by an experienced enthusiast, this manual provides a thorough and detailed restoration guide complete with hundreds of original colour photos. This is the author's third restoration guide, his previous works having been well-received by both professional and amateur restorers alike.

ISBN: 978-1-787111-58-5
Paperback • 27x20.7cm • 208 pages • 600 pictures

For more information and price details, visit our website at www.veloce.co.uk • email: info@veloce.co.uk
• Tel: +44(0)1305 260068

ALSO FROM VELOCE PUBLISHING –

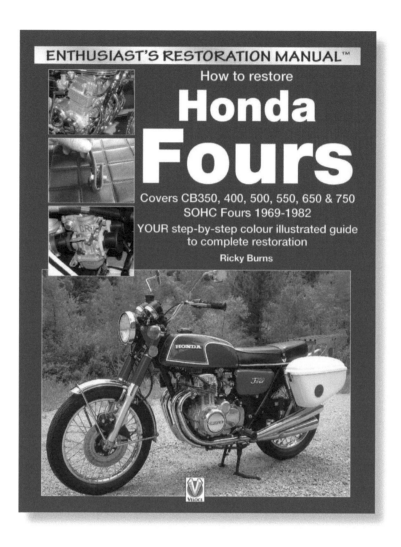

This book gives enthusiasts of the single overhead camshaft Honda Four a step-by-step guide to a full restoration, whether it be the small-but-luxurious CB350/4 right through to the groundbreaking CB750/4. This guide covers dismantling the motorcycle and its components, restoring and sourcing parts, paint spraying, decals and polishing. The chapters cover engine, frame, forks, fuel, exhaust, seat, brakes, tyres, electrics, up to the rebuild and on to safe setup and general maintenance and finally onto riding safely and storage.

ISBN: 978-1-845847-46-3
Paperback • 27x20.7cm • 176 pages • 682 colour pictures

For more information and price details, visit our website at www.veloce.co.uk • email: info@veloce.co.uk
• Tel: +44(0)1305 260068

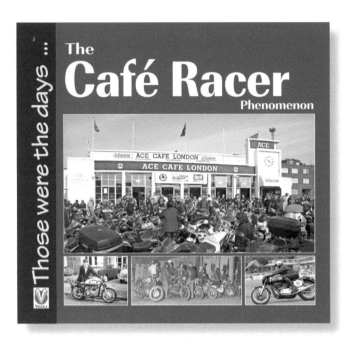

The Café Racer is one of the most enduring styles of motorcycle ever created, capturing the rebellious spirit of the 50s. From original Triton-building Rockers to modern-day Sunday riders on Thruxton 900s, there are thousands of enthusiasts across the world who aspire to own an old school road burner.

A look back at the glory days of the Café Racer, from Friday night dices on the North Circular, through the street specials craze of the Seventies, to the modern day revival. Interviews with some of the old school regulars at the Ace Café, and an in-depth look at the great British bike builders like Norman Hyde, Steve and Lester Harris, the Rickman brothers and Paul Dunstall. Featuring a huge, global Café Racer directory – listing specialist builders, spares suppliers, websites etc – alongside a unique mix of personal memories, unseen photos, iconic machines and chassis builders in profile, this book is a must for any ton-up rider.

ISBN: 978-1-845842-64-2
Paperback • 19x20.5cm • 96 pages
• 100 colour and b&w pictures

A celebration of the sports moped charting the history of a genre created unwittingly by the government in 1972 and killed off by more legislation five years later. This book recaptures the spirit of happy and carefree times and looks at the bikes that gave freedom and mobility to a generation.

ISBN: 978-1-845840-78-5
Paperback • 25x20.7cm • 144 pages • pictures

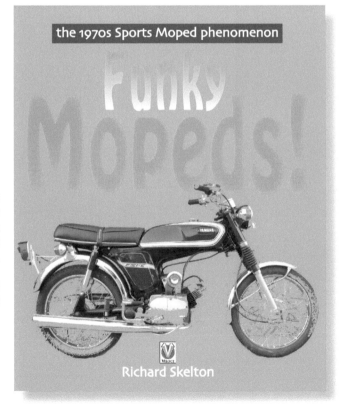

Index